OFFICIAL SOUVENIR GUIDE

THE CITY OF YORK

A UNIQUE GUIDE TO A REMARKABLE CITY

Published by Visit York
www.visityork.org

CITY OF YORK

This book is a celebration of a wonderful city and Visit York would like to acknowledge everyone who has helped in its production.

Our thanks must go to the numerous individuals and organisations who have contributed in different ways and in particular to Andy Bentley for his editorial contributions and support and also to Warwick Burton and Julian Cripps. A special thanks to Dame Judi Dench for her kind introduction.

SOUVENIR GUIDE

Among the organisations who have supplied advice and images are: York Archaeological Trust, Nestle Confectionery Ltd, Yorkshire Tourist Board, City of York Council, Dean and Chapter of York and York Minster Archive Department, Joseph Rowntree Foundation, National Trust, National Railway Museum, National Centre for Early Music, Visit Britain, York Museums Trust and Yorkshire Air Museum.

Published by Visit York, the tourism organisation for the City of York and the surrounding area.

ISBN 978-0-9560309-0-0

CONTENTS

YORK SOUVENIR GUIDE

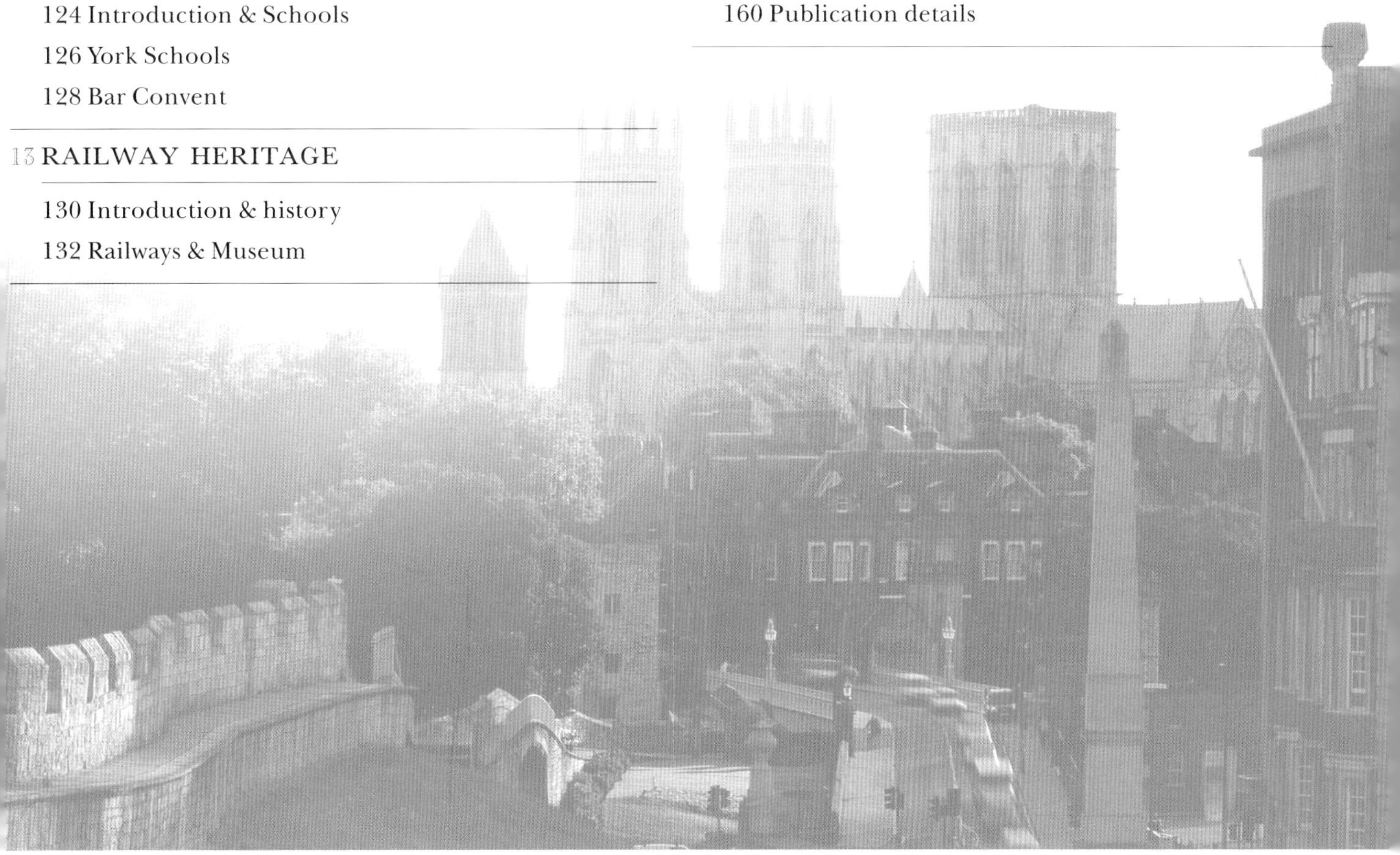

01

PREFACE BY DAME JUDI DENCH

"I was born in York and grew up there, so I have a great fondness for this remarkable city with its winding, cobbled streets and beautiful architecture. I have happy memories of my days at the Mount School and my first appearance in the Mystery Plays. The city has evolved over the years with the arrival of new and exciting attractions, a wealth of interesting shops and a vibrant cafe and evening culture. However, some things never change and, no matter how long I am away, that first glimpse of the magnificent Minster towering above the city will never cease to inspire and move me. I will always be proud to call York my home."

Above: Dame Judi Dench.

Opposite: York Minster in Autumn.
Photographer: Paul Crossman

CITY OF YORK

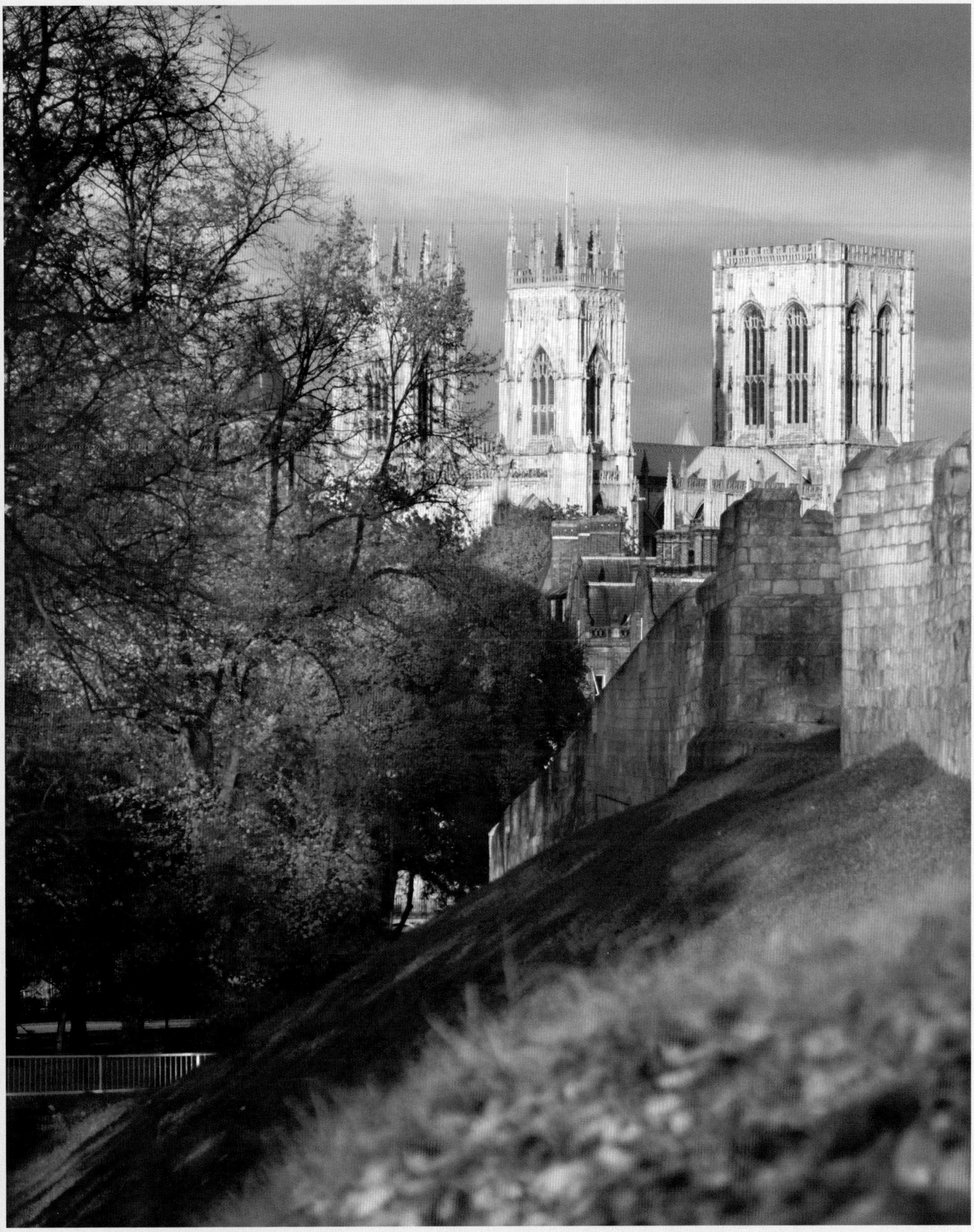

YORK THROUGH THE AGES

THE HISTORY OF YORK TIMELINE PREHISTORIC - 1660s

PREHISTORIC	Area perhaps called 'Eburacon' (meaning 'The Estate of the Eburos' or 'The place where the yew trees grow') by Ancient Britons.
71	City founded by the Romans and named 'EBORACUM' which in 73 becomes the capital of the North of Britannia.
c107	Construction of stone wall enclosing approximately 50 acres.
306	Constantine The Great declared Emperor of Eboracum.
400s	Roman withdrawal leaves city open to Saxon invaders.
627	First Minster built for Saxon King Edwin of Northumbria.
c640	Completion of the first stone Minster dedicated to St. Peter.
700s	City now Saxon capital of Northumbria 'EOFORWIC'.
741	City's second Minster, made of stone, is destroyed by fire.
866	Vikings, under Ivan the Boneless, capture Eoforwic and name it the Viking Kingdom 'Jorvik'.
954	Eric Bloodaxe, last Viking king of Jorvik, dies.
c1000	City known by its present name York.
1020s - 60s	York ruled by powerful Anglo & Scandinavian Earls.
1066	Battles of Fulford and Stamford Bridge weaken Harold's army.
1190	Massacre of city's Jewish community (approx. 150 people) in Clifford's Tower.
1220	Building of present York Minster begins.
1240s - 1340s	Construction of present City Walls.
1314	Edward II decides to base his court in the City of York.
1390s	Richard II wants to make York the capital of England.
1472	York Minster is completed and consecrated.
1486	King Henry VII marries Elizabeth of York, thereby ending the War of the Roses.
1605	Guy Fawkes of York is arrested in London and executed after the foiling of the Gunpowder Plot.
1644	The Great Siege of York by Cromwell's forces.
1660s	Political importance of city gradually starts to decline.

TIMELINE

	THE HISTORY OF YORK TIMELINE 1690s - 2008
1690s	Government now becoming more centralised in London and monarchs very rarely come to York.
1739	Highwayman Dick Turpin is hanged in York.
1829	Arsonist Jonathan Martin sets fire to York Minster.
1839	Railway comes to York.
1840	Accidental fire damages the nave of York Minster.
1907	Substantial Minster restoration programme completed.
1975	Opening of the National Railway Museum, the world's largest collection of trains.
1979	Discovery of buried Viking village which leads to the opening of JORVIK in 1984.
1984	Fire in York Minster destroys south transept roof and Rose Window.
2005	The city hosts Royal Ascot at York, the UK's most prestigious race meeting.
2006	1700th anniversary of Constantine the Great's proclamation as York's Roman Emperor.
2007	York wins European Tourism City of the Year Award.

Clock mounted on St Martin le Grand Church, Coney Street.

YORK THROUGH THE AGES

The Old Bridge over the River Ouse as it stood in August 1809.
Painting by Henry Cave.

INTRODUCTION

As you wander through the streets of this historically rich city, spare a thought for the civilisations that have gone before…

THE ROMANS

While there is archaeological evidence of an iron-age settlement based here earlier, it was the arrival of the Romans – and particularly the famous Ninth Legion – that first created the outpost that eventually became the city of York.

The Roman governor Quintus Petillius Cerialis, presided over southern Britain until, in 71 AD he was dispatched by the Emperor Vespasian from the legion's stronghold at Lincoln to lead his troops north. The reason was to subdue the hostile tribes known as the Brigantes and incorporate the North into the empire. During the journey they set up a temporary camp on a triangle of land between the Rivers Ouse and Foss, a site that provided such an effective natural defence that the camp gradually turned into a more permanent fort. The Romans called their new outpost Eboracum, a name that is thought to mean 'the place of the yew trees'.

Makeshift defences – probably wooden palisades, ditches and dykes – were replaced by more substantial walls of pale limestone, quarried at nearby Tadcaster. At regular intervals the walls were heightened, strengthened and fortified with towers. There were four entrance gates in the outer wall, each fortification controlling one of the main roads into the garrison.

Above & Opposite: The Multangular Tower in Museum Gardens - the only Roman tower still in existence in the city.

YORK THROUGH THE AGES

THE ROMANS

Within a hundred years Eboracum had become an important settlement, with more than 5,000 troops garrisoned. The site was so strategically important for quelling rebellious northern tribes, that the Roman city became the main military headquarters in the north of Britain.

The fortress was of the typically Roman playing-card shape; rectangular with rounded corners – occupying a fifty-acre site. The Romans built the first bridge spanning the River Ouse, though not on the site of any of today's bridges and, despite what some visitors imagine, the city walls that are walked today are not of Roman origin. Some remains of the Roman fortifications lie under the current walls between the Multangular Tower and just past Monk Bar.

Though many Roman artefacts have been unearthed, very few structural remains of Roman Eboracum have survived. The city, defined from its very beginnings by its boundary walls, changed over centuries as new buildings were erected on older foundations. It now takes major archaeological work to find evidence of Roman buildings. Successive layers of stonework, beginning from Roman times, can be seen behind the public library, in the ramparts of the city wall. The base of the nearby Multangular Tower in the Museum Gardens is Roman with medieval additions on top. A Roman column, now re-erected opposite the Minster, is a potent reminder that a huge Roman hall (the Basilica of the Principia) once occupied the site where the Minster now stands. The Roman Baths, a pub in St Sampson's Square, has the remains of a Roman bathhouse deep in its basement.

Above: The Roman Baths, a pub in St Sampson's Square, has the remains of a Roman bathhouse deep in its basement.

Opposite: York's Roman history is frequently celebrated with festivals and re-enactments.

YORK THROUGH THE AGES

THE ROMANS

In 197AD the Northern Tribes threatened Eboracum and the fort was rebuilt in stone in around 211AD. Its military importance grew, making Eboracum a major military site in the country. The population of 5,000 soldiers was supplemented by family members, slaves and the administrators required for the smooth running of the garrison. To meet its further needs, a large civilian population of merchants and craftspeople grew up - some outside the walls but most living in the walled Colonia in the Micklegate area.

We know that the original fort was about 475 metres long and 400 metres wide, butting up to the northern bank of the River Ouse. The layout followed the grid-pattern common to other Roman forts and the most important public building was the military headquarters, the Principia. From here stemmed two major streets, the Via Praetoria and Via Principalis, which correspond roughly to the streets known today as Stonegate and Petergate. The Via Praetoria extended down to the river, spanned by a wooden bridge; the road then continued to become the main route to the south, exiting the city at a point close to Micklegate Bar.

Settlements grew up alongside the roads and by 213AD, Eboracum had expanded to the point where it was designated a Colonia, raising it to a status already shared by the Roman forts at Gloucester, Lincoln and Colchester.

We can imagine a bustling, cosmopolitan garrison and city, though its permanence proved to be an illusion. At the very height of its prominence, Eboracum was abandoned. The north had never been completely subdued and in 410AD the Romans decided that this distant outpost of the Roman Empire was becoming too problematic and legions were recalled from Britain.

Constantine

By the early 4th century, York had reached the height of its power, wealth and influence.

When the Roman Emperor Constantius Chlorus died in York in 306AD he was succeeded by his son, Constantine. The new emperor returned to his homeland and it was there, in 312AD, after a decisive battle at the Milvian Bridge, close to Rome that it is said he saw the sign of a cross and felt the power of Christ. As a result of his victory, Constantine legalised Christianity and became the first Christian emperor. He died in 337AD and was buried in his new capital of the Roman Empire – Constantinople.

Today, the statue of Constantine stands outside the Minster and shows him contemplating a cross formed by a sword broken in battle.

Right: This 4th century stone head of Constantine was found in Stonegate in 1860 by workmen digging a sewer.

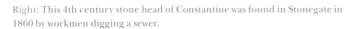

Opposite: Roman column outside York Minster. Some say that the column is upside down, which causes amusement, but this is strongly denied!

YORK THROUGH THE AGES

THE ANGLO SAXONS

The withdrawal of the Romans left a huge cultural gap which the warring British tribes were unable to fill. The administrative orderliness that characterised the Roman occupation was slowly unwound and Hadrian's Wall, now undefended, offered no resistance to the Picts. Centralised government disappeared to be replaced by scattered kingdoms. The centuries that followed are often called the Dark Ages, though the period of time between the Roman withdrawal and the Viking invasions probably saw York's greatest expansion.

Anglo Saxon adventurers left their homelands in Northern Germany and sailed up the Humber Estuary. By the 6th century most of the north of England was in Anglo Saxon hands with the area being divided into two kingdoms: Bernicia comprised land north of the River Tees, while Deira, a name meaning the kingdom of the waters, extended as far south as the Humber. York was adopted as its capital and given the name of Eoforwic.

The Dark Ages are poorly documented and in the absence of facts, a shadowy period of myths and legends has developed. We do know that the two kingdoms came to blows, before eventually combining in 620AD to become the powerful Anglo-Saxon kingdom of Northumbria.

The Anglo Saxon occupation of York was unusual in that the Germanic invaders usually built new settlements. An impression of York as it would have been has to be conjured up in the imagination: the Anglo Saxons generally built in wood and few of their buildings have survived, apart from the remains of some stone fortifications. It was during this period that the English Christian church was established and in 625AD King Edwin of Northumbria married Princess Ethelburga who had embraced Christianity. In 627AD the King himself was baptised into the faith and for the ceremony he hastily erected a modest wooden church near to the spot the Minster would later occupy. While Edwin re-established York as the capital of his kingdom, his queen ensured that York also became the ecclesiastical centre.

Despite the social upheavals that characterised the next two centuries, York prospered as a religious centre benefiting particularly from the influence of two powerful figures: St Wilfrid and Archbishop Egbert. It was after a fire, one of many that York was to suffer, that Archbishop Egbert rebuilt the wooden Minster.

Christianity also brought learning to York. In the eighth century, the great scholar Alcuin was Master of the School of St Peter which received students from all over England. By the time he left Britain to become Master of Emperor Charlemagne's Palace School at Aachen, Eoforwic was the most important centre of learning in this part of Britain.

In the church hierarchy, York became equal in importance to Canterbury; a position of religious eminence the city still occupies today.

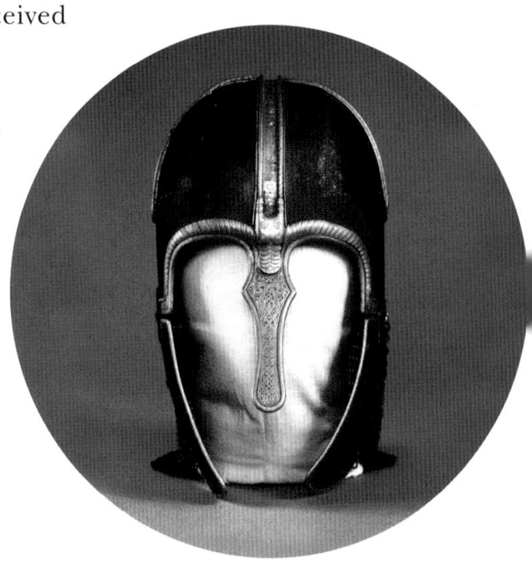

Right: This famous 8th century Coppergate helmet carries the inscription of its owner 'Oshere' together with a prayer.
Courtesy of York Archaeological Trust.

Opposite: Virgin and Child c.1150 is thought to be one of the few remaining relics from the Saxon Minster
Copyright Dean and Chapter of York and Jarrold Publishing.

YORK THROUGH THE AGES

THE VIKINGS

This golden age was short-lived and by the middle years of the 9th century, Northumbria was becoming susceptible to isolated raids by Danish pirates. Prosperous York was an obvious target for the Viking invaders and in 866 a huge armada sailed up the tidal River Ouse.

With the Kingdom of Northumbria riven by feuds, the Viking hordes found the city inadequately defended and overran it with little opposition. The invaders had no greater ambition other than the 'raping and pillaging' for which they are more often remembered. They entered York and finding that it would make an ideal base for further incursions, strengthened its defences. They adapted the city's Anglo-Saxon name to something that sounded easier on the Scandinavian ear: Eoforwic became Jorvik. Truly the Vikings were here to stay.

It is difficult to establish just how deserved the Vikings' reputation for murderous ferocity actually was. Certainly they took York by force and ransacked other towns for goods they could plunder. Yet their tenure of northern England is marked by a willingness to negotiate with the indigenous population. Many Vikings embraced Christianity.

The Danes who settled in York were industrious people and, intent on making Jorvik the Viking Capital of Northumbria, continued the tradition of trade that had already made the town prosperous.

Viking York was a bustling town of squat houses, constructed of wood and wattle, and inhabited by craftsmen and traders in a frantic environment of noise and grime. When the Vikings' grip on England was finally loosened in the 10th Century, England became a unified kingdom. Viking kings still ruled from York, but their power was diminished. The last Viking king – Erik Bloodaxe, was murdered, appropriately enough with an axe, in 954.

Top of page: A hoard of Viking coins.
Courtesy of York Archaeological Trust.

Opposite: York celebrates its Viking connection with a festival each February.

YORK THROUGH THE AGES

THE NORMANS

As every schoolchild knows, the Battle of Hastings was fought in 1066. However, what many don't realise, is that in the September of that same year, the English were defeated at the Battle of Fulford, just south of York. This was followed five days later by an even bloodier confrontation to the east of the city at the Battle of Stamford Bridge where Harold, the last of the Saxon kings, defeated an army brought together by his own rebellious brother, Tostig, and King Hardrada of Norway. It proved to be a short-lived victory. Depleted and exhausted, Harold's troops then made the long march south to meet the invading forces of Duke William of Normandy at Hastings. Harold was killed by an arrow through his eye and the victorious William led his army north to York.

William met little resistance from the York people and was given the keys to the city. In turn, he made it his military headquarters and put down a couple of Viking uprisings and built fortifications which have lasted to the present day. On two mounds, one each side of the river, he built a motte and bailey castle. The mound to the north was later the site of Clifford's Tower whereas Baille Hill, south of the river and adjacent to the city wall, is now bare.

The second Viking raid saw York in flames and the Norman garrison defeated. William's response was swift and merciless. He recaptured the city and – in a two year act of vengeance known as the Harrying of the North – destroyed villages, farms and crops. Of those who survived the massacre, many succumbed to the famine that resulted.

The Domesday Book, compiled in 1086, records that York's population had declined from 8,000 to 2,000, and the entire region between York and Durham was summed up, succinctly, as 'wasteland'. Yet before the Norman invasion, York had been called "as beautiful as Rome".

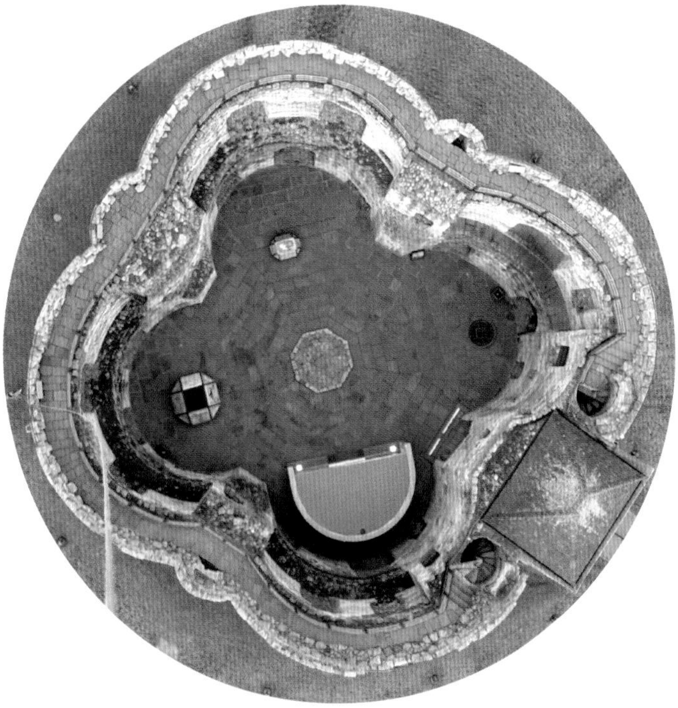

Above: Aerial view of Clifford's Tower.

Opposite: Clifford's Tower in the mist.

YORK THROUGH THE AGES

THE NORMANS

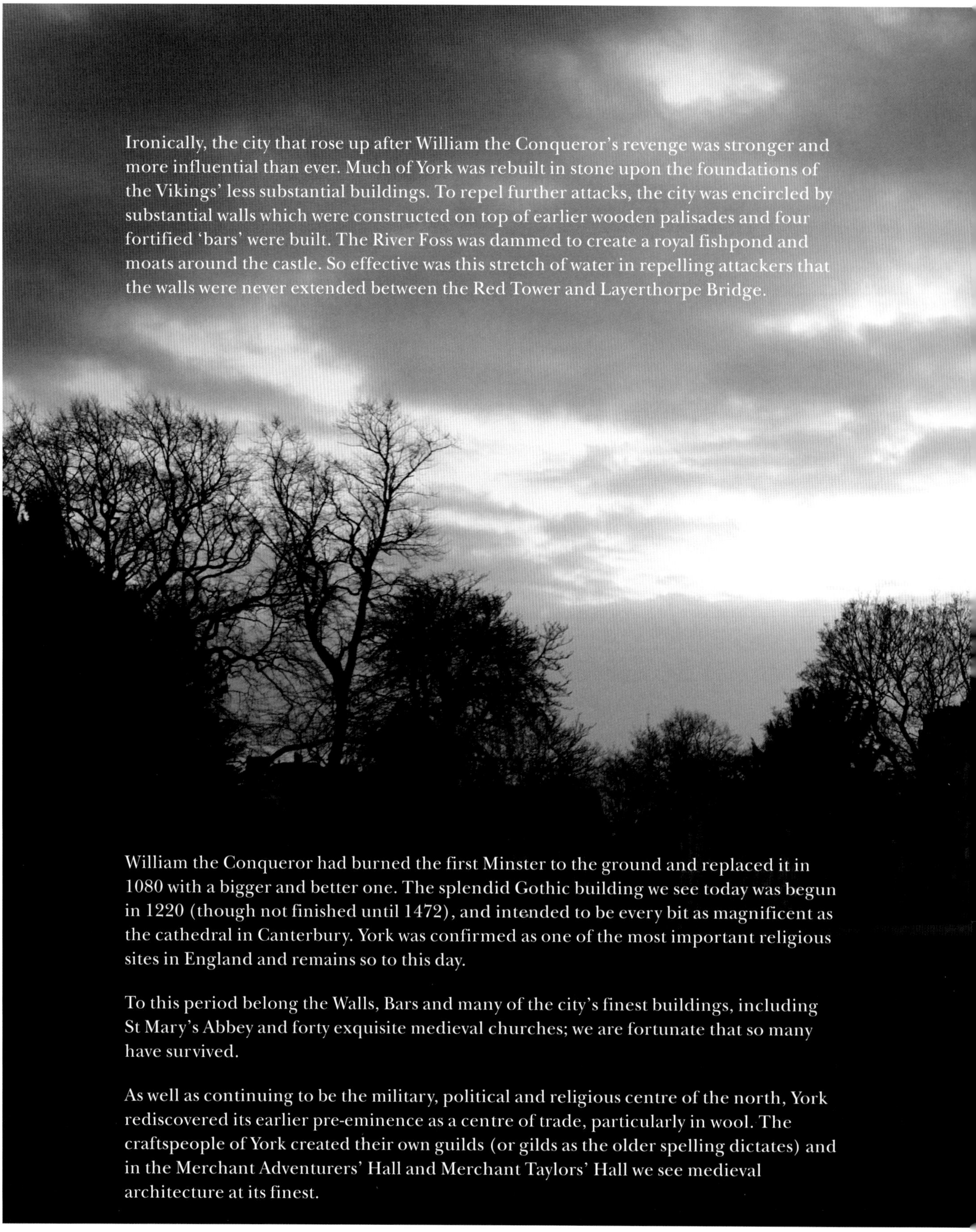

Ironically, the city that rose up after William the Conqueror's revenge was stronger and more influential than ever. Much of York was rebuilt in stone upon the foundations of the Vikings' less substantial buildings. To repel further attacks, the city was encircled by substantial walls which were constructed on top of earlier wooden palisades and four fortified 'bars' were built. The River Foss was dammed to create a royal fishpond and moats around the castle. So effective was this stretch of water in repelling attackers that the walls were never extended between the Red Tower and Layerthorpe Bridge.

William the Conqueror had burned the first Minster to the ground and replaced it in 1080 with a bigger and better one. The splendid Gothic building we see today was begun in 1220 (though not finished until 1472), and intended to be every bit as magnificent as the cathedral in Canterbury. York was confirmed as one of the most important religious sites in England and remains so to this day.

To this period belong the Walls, Bars and many of the city's finest buildings, including St Mary's Abbey and forty exquisite medieval churches; we are fortunate that so many have survived.

As well as continuing to be the military, political and religious centre of the north, York rediscovered its earlier pre-eminence as a centre of trade, particularly in wool. The craftspeople of York created their own guilds (or gilds as the older spelling dictates) and in the Merchant Adventurers' Hall and Merchant Taylors' Hall we see medieval architecture at its finest.

YORK THROUGH THE AGES

St Mary's Abbey, Museum Gardens.

TUDORS & STUARTS

The second half of the 15th century proved a difficult time for the city. General unrest in the North among the population and a fierce hatred between the houses of York and Lancaster led to a series of battles that lasted for over 30 years (1451 - 1485). Known as the Wars of the Roses – derived from the two emblems, the white rose of York and the red rose of Lancaster, both factions struggled for overall power. The conflict was economically disastrous for the country and its influence with France. There were no victors, the House of Plantagenet collapsed and was replaced by the House of Tudor.

War with France decimated exports and caused York to lose what had been its monopoly in the wool trade. In 1533, Henry VIII broke away from Rome and established the Church of England, putting himself at the head and triggering the 'Reformation'. This saw the Dissolution of the Monasteries throughout the country with York losing its abbey, priories and friaries and its religious communities surrendering their power. Ironically, many of the city's most historic, non-religious buildings came through the succeeding centuries largely unscathed.

Although York suffered greatly at the hands of Henry VIII, he did do the city a great service by re-establishing the Council of the North in the former house of the Abbot of St Mary's (today's King's Manor). This became the Council's administrative centre and during the reigns of Elizabeth I and James I, its importance led to York's revival – it was to become an important city once again.

Parliament disbanded the Council in 1641 but Charles I made York his capital for a time, establishing a printing press in St William's College and the Royal Mint nearby. Charles left York in 1642 after it became apparent there was to be a civil war.

Above: Henry VIII

Opposite: St William's College

YORK THROUGH THE AGES

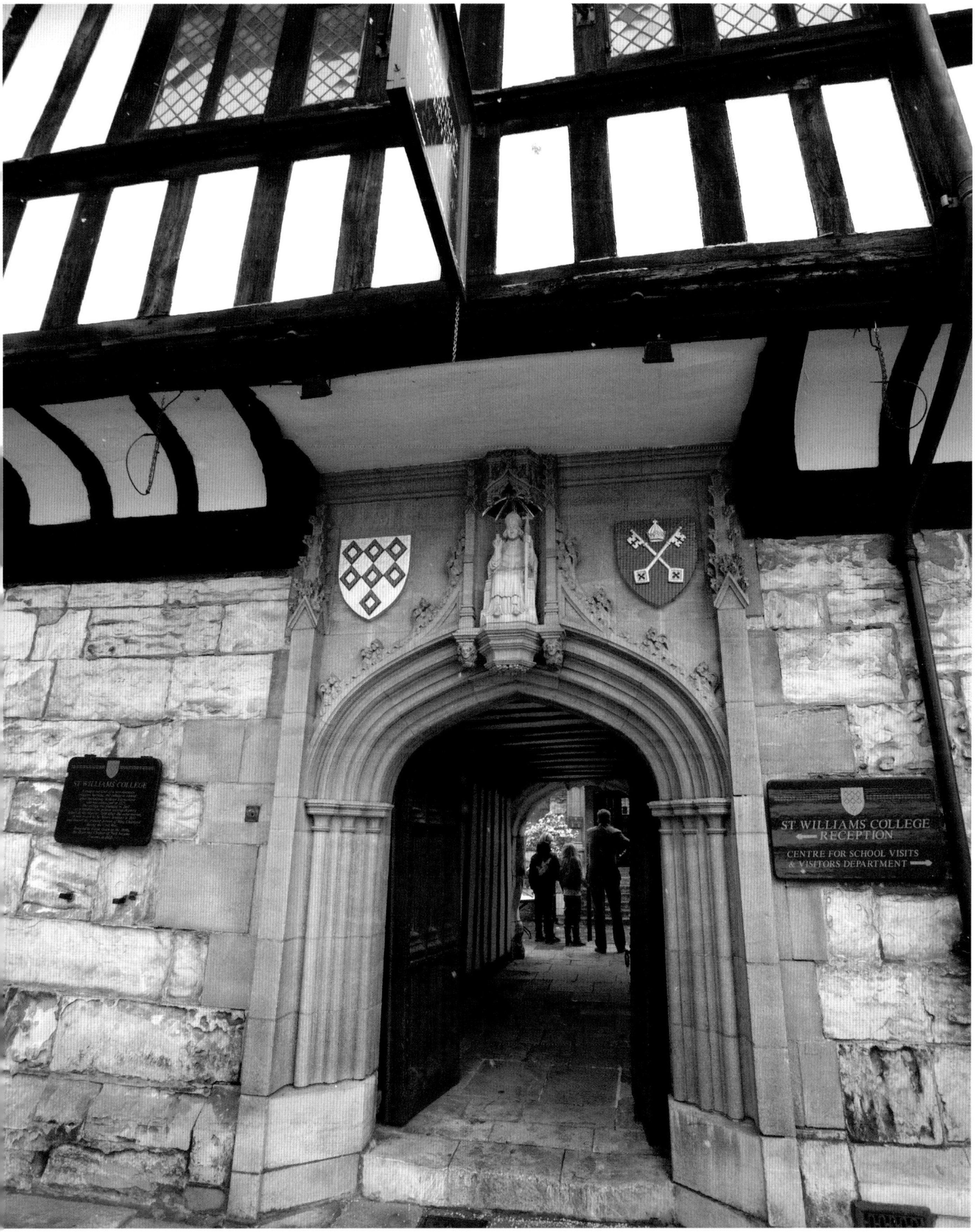

THE CIVIL WAR

Civil War erupted in 1642 with the Parliamentary army of 30,000 meeting Royalist forces at Marston Moor. The Parliamentarians won the battle and, in April 1644, an army commanded by Sir Thomas Fairfax besieged York for three months. Charles I's nephew Prince Rupert was sent to help and heading an army of around 15 000 men, he forced Fairfax's troops to break off the siege and retreat. They turned on him at Marston Moor where Rupert and the Royalists suffered a crushing defeat.

The siege was renewed and lasted until 15 June 1644 when the city surrendered. Lord Fairfax, a Yorkshireman, gave orders to his troops that nothing was to be destroyed. It was he and his son's intervention that prevented the destruction of York's fine buildings.

York entered the 18th century as a peaceful and elegant city with a fine legacy of Georgian buildings.

Above: Helmet, c.1630.

Opposite: The Surrender of York to the Roundheads.
Oil painting by Ernest Crofts. Courtesy of Sotheby's Picture Library.

YORK THROUGH THE AGES

VICTORIAN TO GEORGIAN

The 18th century saw York flourish as a fashionable centre for society. It became something of a rich person's playground with the wealthy arriving from London to be diverted and entertained. Thankfully, by 1839, this journey took only 21 hours by stagecoach compared to the four wretchedly uncomfortable days travellers had been subjected to in the past.

The emphasis at this time was on leisure and luxury, with visitors frequenting York's theatres, taverns and law courts all in the name of amusement. The races were in their heyday and public hangings at Clifford's Tower and the Knavesmire were a much loved attraction, often drawing in crowds in excess of 10,000.

Lavish, elaborate balls were held in the Assembly Rooms and fashionable society would gather to see and be seen. Tobias Smollett in his novel, 'The Exhibition of Humphrey Clinker' writes of these events, "...the company, on a ball-night, must look like an assembly of fantastic fairies, reveling by moonlight among the columns of a Grecian temple."

One of the reasons people came to York was to escape the effects of industry which brought noise, smells and pollution to the major cities of England. On the whole, industrialisation passed York by. Here was a city with no coal and insufficient water power to drive water wheels. The city was able to preserve its heritage and people came to admire the architecture and socialise.

The city did, however, enjoy the benefits of two key industries. George Hudson, the then Lord Mayor, brought the railway to York in 1839, thereby guaranteeing the city's commercial wealth for years to come. His foresight regarding the development of rail communications boosted York's other major industry – chocolate – which established the city as Britain's 'confectionery capital' for 150 years.

Paradoxically, developments in road and rail led to the city's decline and whilst rail improvements brought in everyday visitors, the wealthy aristocrats now found it easy to head south to London.

Opposite: Fairfax House –
believed to be the finest Georgian townhouse in England.

YORK THROUGH THE AGES

HISTORIC STREETS

Based on a Roman settlement, the centre of York is remarkably compact which means that walking from one side of the city centre to the other is easy and pleasurable

York - Where the streets are gates, the gates are bars and the bars are pubs!

Hidden within the tangle of York's narrow streets and snickelways are clues to its diverse history. Stroll along Stonegate or Petergate and you will be following the Roman thoroughfares that led away from the Principia, where now stands the Minster. The name 'gate' however, came not from the Romans but from the Viking word for 'street'. This influence can be seen too in numerous villages whose names end in 'thorpe', a suffix derived from the Scandinavian word for a village.

Some of York's street names have obvious derivations. Monkgate was the street of the monks; Swinegate was, until the 17th century, the site of a pig market; Tanner Row was where the city's leather industry was concentrated and Coffee Yard was the site of York's first coffee house.

Other names need some linguistic unravelling. Aldwark, for example, indicates an old fortification and Spurriergate was the street of the spur-makers. Bootham was where market traders would set up their stalls or 'booths'; Micklegate meant 'the Great Street' and Gillygate recalls a church – dedicated to St Giles – which has long since disappeared.

Other streets bear the names of some of York's more prominent citizens. George Hudson Street, formerly Railway Street, recognises the man hailed as the 'Railway King' whereas Leeman Road honours George Leeman, who succeeded Hudson as Lord Mayor of York.

In recent years the city has faced an uneasy relationship with the motor car, though the ring road, pedestrianisation and 'park & ride' schemes have solved the worst of the traffic problems. The city has embraced the bicycle and a network of cycle paths allow both visitors and residents to enjoy leisurely rides.

Opposite: Shambles at night.

INTRODUCTION

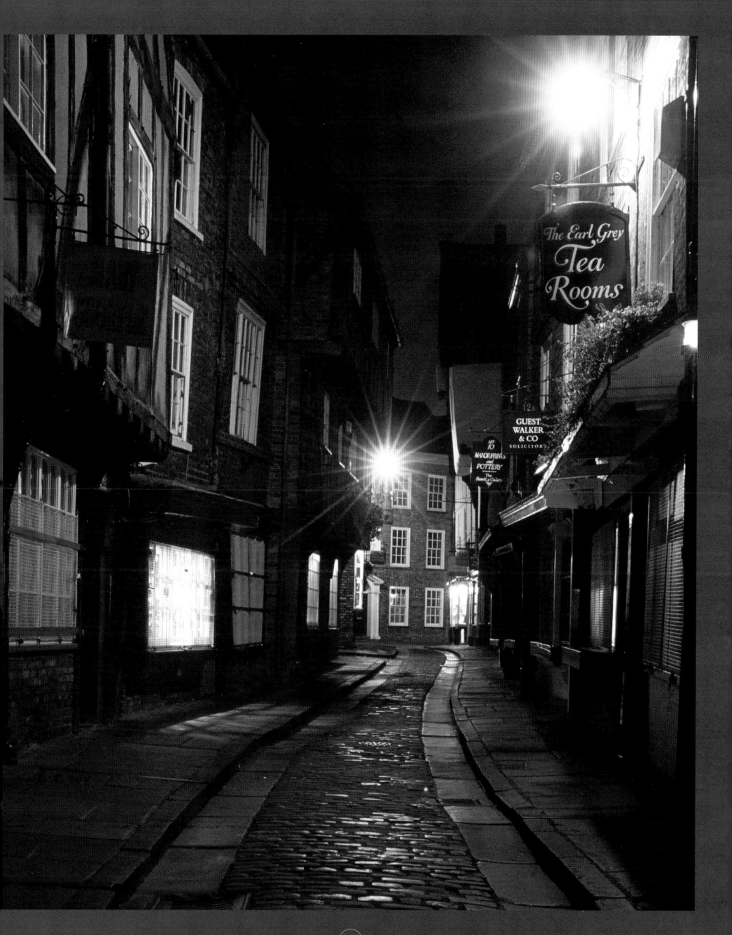

SHAMBLES

Many towns still have shambles (the name traditionally given to streets of butchers' shops and slaughter-houses) but none can match the Shambles of York, arguably the best-preserved in the country. It is the only street in York to have been mentioned in the Domesday Book of 1086 and William the Conqueror's half-brother is mentioned within its pages as a stall-holder. The butchers' guild was one of the largest in York and bizarrely had responsibility for running the city's prison.

Though none of the original shop-fronts have survived from Medieval times, some properties still have exterior wooden shelves: reminders of when cuts of meat were served from the open windows. Joints of meat, poultry and game would have been suspended from hooks.

The street was made narrow by design, thus keeping the meat out of direct sunlight. It is not hard to imagine this little thoroughfare thronged with people and awash with offal and discarded bones; the smell on a hot day must have been overpowering. The outbreaks of plague which periodically erupted in the city may be blamed on such unsanitary practices.

The home of Margaret Clitherow

At number 35 is a little house dedicated to the memory of Margaret Clitherow who was born in 1556 and lived with her husband in the Shambles. At this time, practising the Roman Catholic faith was banned in England but Margaret, a staunch Catholic, would use her attic room to harbour Catholic priests, smuggling them in and out under cover of darkness. In 1586 she was caught and tried at York Assizes. She refused to plead at her trial and was sentenced to the brutal punishment of being crushed to death by having a wooden door placed on top of her on which were piled heavy rocks. The remains of one of her hands is preserved today in the Bar Convent on Blossom Street.

Above: A plaque dedicated to Margaret Clitherow 1556 – 1586.

Opposite: Shoppers in Shambles.

HISTORIC STREETS

STONEGATE

The street of printers

This is unquestionably one of the most beautiful streets in the country and follows the route taken by the main road between the Roman garrison and the Roman headquarters (Principia) on the site of the Minster. No relics of the Roman thoroughfare remain but Stonegate retains much of its medieval character and there are a number of interesting architectural features which are worth looking out for.

A strikingly painted beam which spans the street was first put up in 1733 and directs travellers to Ye Olde Starre Inne, probably the city's oldest surviving public house. The name itself is believed to have been given to this heritage tavern by Royalists in honour of King Charles I who was warmly nicknamed the 'Old Star'.

A carved printer's devil, painted an appropriate scarlet, squats under the eaves of number 33 at the junction with Coffee Yard. The first of many York printers opened here in 1480 and the figure is a reminder that the youngest apprentice who had the job of carrying hot type in a print-shop, was nick-named a 'printers' devil' – a reference no doubt to them being mischief makers.

Stonegate rapidly became known as the street of printers with the earliest known book being printed in 1509. For a time during the 1600s, York was one of only three places outside of London permitted to print – the other two being Oxford and Cambridge. This led to documentation originating from this street that would, over time, change the course of history. In 1649 Thomas Broad printed a justification for the beheading of Charles I and in 1688, John Waite took an enormous risk in printing William of Orange's historic manifesto against King James II. He gambled successfully and was awarded the status of a Royal printer by William and Mary.

Thomas Gent, Stonegate's last prominent printer, was the first to print 'Chap books' (also known as Penny Histories) during the mid 18th century. These small books had become very popular in the country as reading material for poorer people. They concentrated on Bible stories, fairy stories and nursery rhymes although Gent mainly printed Bible stories. The popularity of these cheaply priced booklets show that the level of literacy was wider than is often assumed for this period.

As a natural progression from printing, Stonegate soon saw the opening of many bookshops and these played a prominent role in commissioning publications. At number 35, another shop sign, that of a bible with the date 1682, can still be seen. It was from this very shop that Laurence Sterne's novel, Tristram Shandy, was published in 1760.

Above: The printer's devil.

Opposite: Stonegate.

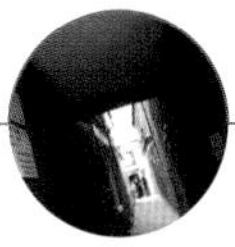

HISTORIC STREETS

PETERGATE

Named after St Peter, the patron saint of the Minster, Petergate is an exceptionally long street comprising two halves - High and Low Petergate. It follows the route of the main thoroughfare in the Roman fortress of Eboracum when it was the 'Via Principalis' – the main cross street. At each end, on the sites of Bootham Bar and King's Square, would have been gates to the Roman fortress.

Today, Petergate is one of the city's most popular shopping areas, its architecture being an assortment of Medieval, Georgian and Victorian. Look out for the figure of an American Indian at 76 Low Petergate. The boy's skirt and headdress represent tobacco leaves and would have advertised a tobacconist's shop - now long gone. High up on the walls can still be seen a number of plaques known as 'firemarks'. These were erected during the 18th and 19th centuries by insurance companies, with their own fire brigades, to identify the properties that they had insured. Denoting the sign of a bookseller, the figure of Minerva at the junction of Minster Gates shows the Roman goddess of wisdom and drama leaning on a pile of books. Beside her are an owl and a theatrical mask of tragedy. It was at this bookshop that authors and literary readers would meet as members of the York Book Club.

The vicinity was popular with booksellers and book-binders during the late 17th and 18th century and Minster Gate became known locally as '*bookbinders*' alley'...

Above: Minerva, the Roman Godess of Wisdom.

HISTORIC STREETS

CONEY STREET & ST HELEN'S SQUARE

...*the King's* Highway

Coney Street, extending from Ousegate to St Helen's Square, is one of the few thoroughfares in York to have kept the Anglo Saxon word 'Strete' meaning the King's Highway. It follows the path of the Roman civilian street which ran between the fortress and the River Ouse. (Contrary to what many people think, 'coney' in this context means king and not rabbit!)

Over the centuries, the accumulation of domestic refuse has caused the ground level to rise by as much as 20 feet, rendering this street safe from river flooding. Most of the distinguished buildings have been lost to retail development, making Coney Street one of the city's most popular shopping areas.

Many of the old public houses have also been crowded out by shops but two are commemorated by plaques; the Black Swan Inn and the George Inn. Anne and Charlotte Bronte stayed in the latter in 1849 on their way to Scarborough where Anne died.

The partially ruined 15th century church of St Martin-le-Grand stands largely unnoticed today. Its clock, topped with the figure of 'the Little Admiral' is a familiar landmark and this 1940's model replaces the original clock of 1688. The church was severely damaged by German bombers on a night in 1942 that claimed 80 lives in the city. The Guildhall too received a direct hit and was burnt out by incendiaries. It was rebuilt to its original design and re-opened in 1960 by the Queen Mother. The exterior is best appreciated from across the River Ouse.

St Helen's Square was, until 1733, part of the graveyard of St Helen's Church, a building which still occupies one corner of the square. Here too can be found the Mansion House, the splendid Georgian residence of the city's Lord Mayors during their periods of office. It is one of only a small handful of Mansion Houses in the country which provides this residential function. Built in 1725-26, with the interior completed in 1732, the Mansion House pre-dates London's by 21 years.

Left: The restored clock mounted on the side of St Martin le Grand has become a well known Coney Street landmark. The character on top, which has survived from an earlier 'Little Admiral'; shows the naval figure pointing a cross staff (an early form of sextant) at the sun to check his position. On the side of the clock is the gilded head of Father Time.

Opposite: Mansion House.

HISTORIC STREETS

GRAPE LANE & SWINEGATE

...a street of sin

A cursory glance at a street map shows that the city's larger thoroughfares create a square, inside which is a labyrinth of lanes and ginnels. Two of these, Swinegate and Grape Lane were, in medieval times, at the centre of a busy trading area.

Named after its pig market, Swinegate would reverberate with sounds of squealing livestock as they were brought, penned, bought and sold in this enclosed space. Market traders had to pay a toll to the city Corporation to sell their wares which led to the practice of trading in the nearby streets to the market itself in order to avoid the toll. Hence the expression 'forestalling'.

The etymology of the name 'Grape' regarding Grape Lane is entertaining. In medieval times 'grap' meant 'grope' and the street became known as 'Grope Lane'. As a street of 'sin' the city's inhabitants had simply given it an appropriate trade name and it must be concluded that the medieval prostitutes were trading reasonably well to be recognised in this way!

Perhaps the most intriguing medieval ginnel in York runs off Grape Lane creating a short cut into Stonegate. Coffee Yard is over seventy metres long and is a combination of a common lane, yard and tunnel. In the ginnel's yard is Barley Hall, the restored medieval residence of Alderman Snawsell, a former Lord Mayor of York and a goldsmith.

In the early 1990's, Swinegate and Grape Lane were extensively but sympathetically re-developed. They retain a relaxed atmosphere, ideal for browsing the speciality shops, stylish restaurants and wine bars.

Above: Ice sculpture as part of York's annual Festival of Angels.

Opposite: Wrought iron work in Swinegate.

HISTORIC STREETS

COPPERGATE

It is no exaggeration to say that Coppergate – the street and its name – has been revitalised by the development of a modern shopping centre. Tastefully designed, it has won several awards and its square and surrounding shops have added vitality to the street.

The archaeological discovery in the early 1970's of a Viking settlement during the construction of the shopping centre, has brought pertinency to the street name itself. Coppergate is derived from the Scandinavian word 'koppari' and is a trade name meaning the street of the cup maker. The five year archaeological dig unearthed some of the tools that the craftsmen would have used and which were so vital to their way of life.

Being situated on the banks of the River Foss, the Viking settlement had been well preserved in the waterlogged soil and comprised an intricate maze of houses, workshops and alleyways. The excavations also uncovered the largest collection of 10th century artefacts ever found in Britain, including a superb Anglo-Saxon helmet.

Coppergate around the year 950 was one of the busiest streets in Viking York. We now know that the Jorvik folk wore colourful woollen clothes and intricate jewellery, played board games and traded their wares at market stalls along this street.
Innovatively, a museum was built on the site to house the archaeologists' finds and today the JORVIK Viking Centre displays hundreds of excavated items including utensils, tools and even clothing. This award-winning museum also dramatically depicts life in Viking York through the reconstruction, in actual size, of a Viking village - right down to the sounds and smells.

Top of page: Viking beads.
Courtesy of York Archaeological Trust.

Opposite: Coppergate Shopping.

HISTORIC STREETS

GOODRAMGATE

Possibly named after Guthrum, a Viking chieftain who led his army into York in the year 878, Goodramgate contains the oldest row of houses in the city. Named Lady Row, these houses date from the early 14th century and were originally occupied by priests. They are among the country's earliest surviving example of houses with overhanging jetties - the top floor projects over the lower as a way of avoiding tax that was only charged on ground floor area.

The half timbered building bridging a path at the road's junction with College Street is all that remains of a covered bridge used by the Vicars Choral to walk to the Minster from their lodgings in Bedern – thereby avoiding the temptations of the street! Tucked behind Lady Row, and accessible by a gate that's easy to miss, is Holy Trinity. One of York's finest medieval churches, its little churchyard, hemmed in by buildings on all sides, provides an oasis of calm away from the bustling streets.

Above & opposite: Goodramgate contains the oldest row of houses in the city.

HISTORIC STREETS

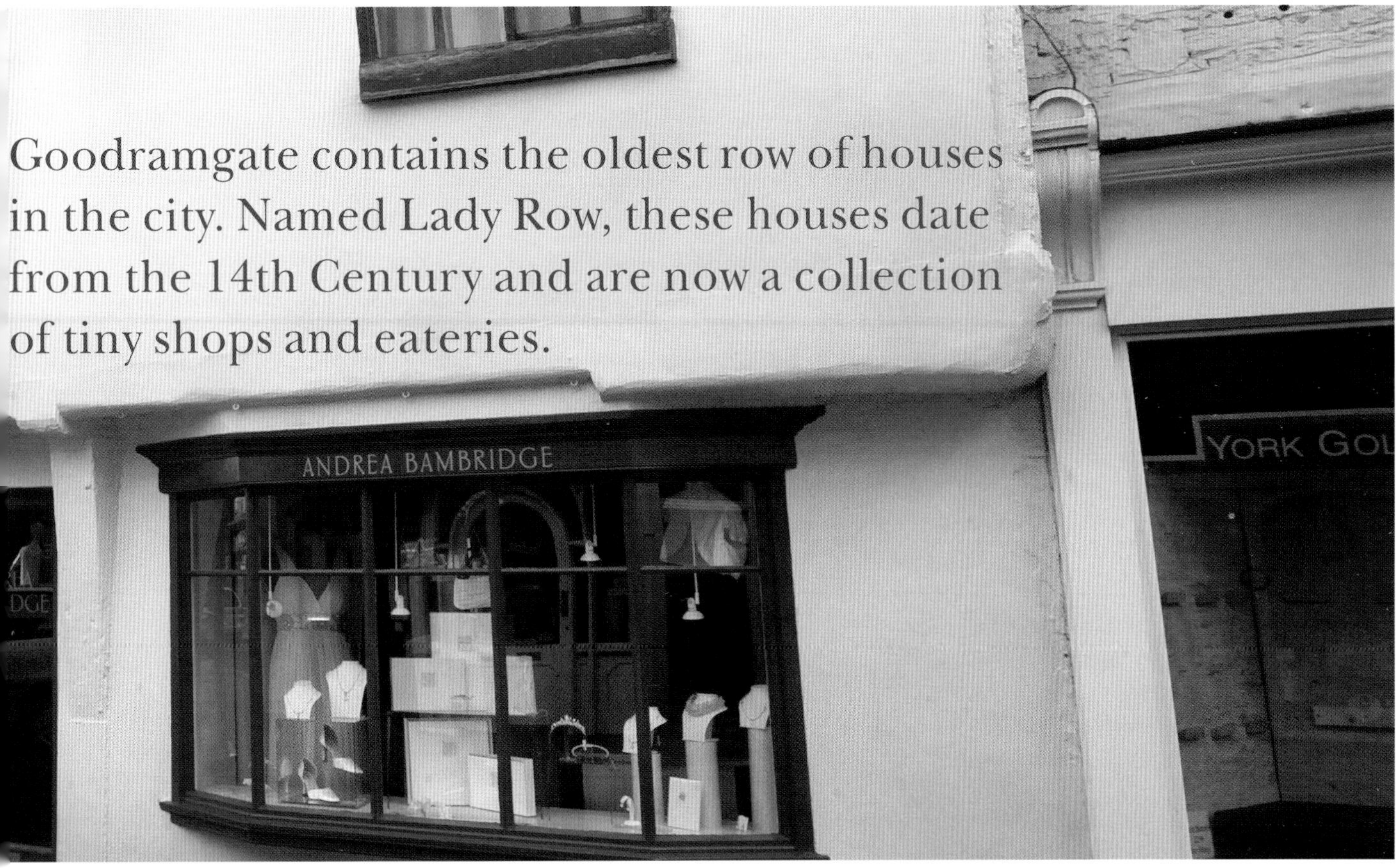

Goodramgate contains the oldest row of houses in the city. Named Lady Row, these houses date from the 14th Century and are now a collection of tiny shops and eateries.

...all that remains of a covered way used by choristers...

MICKLEGATE

With a name meaning 'Great Street' and an imposing Bar at its entrance, Micklegate provides fitting access to the city from the south. From the 14th century, visiting monarchs were greeted by the city's dignitaries at Micklegate Bar and as a warning to those who wished to enter the city via this thoroughfare, heads of traitors were impaled on top of the battlements.

Micklegate has had a mix of residential and commercial properties and its trading wealth is reflected by the great timber framed houses built in the 15th and 16th centuries. The plague of 1550-1551 took hold in lower Micklegate resulting in a lot of small tenements coming onto the market at knock-down prices, which were bought for site value and development.

The street scene we see today is largely due to another building boom in the Georgian period (1720-1820) when wealthy families, visiting the city during the 'season', commissioned the building of substantial town houses or added Georgian façades to medieval structures.

During the Victorian period, many residences were converted into the shops that we see today. No 94 is on the site of one of York's numerous coaching inns. In 1846 it was fitted out as a dram shop – pioneering in York a new style of counter service and stand-up beer drinking which was common in London. Typically, a 'dram shop' had two public rooms off a side passage.

Micklegate is also distinguished by three churches. First mentioned in 1194, the church of St John the Evangelist closed in 1934 but lives on as a popular wine bar. The church of St Martin-Cum-Gregory is mentioned in the Domesday Book of 1086, its tower being rebuilt in 1844. Whilst it holds notable furnishings, it also houses glass by the important York glass painter, William Peckitt, who was buried in the church's chancel in 1795.

The church of Holy Trinity has a complex history with the first structure being destroyed in the great fire in 1137. The priory church had much prominence in Micklegate, becoming a parish church after the Act of Dissolution of 1535.

Right: A fine example of Joseph Hansom's pioneering invention, the Hansom Cab, can be seen in the Castle Museum.

Opposite: Micklegate.

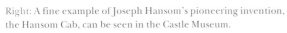

HISTORIC STREETS

No 114 is the birthplace of Joseph Hansom, the inventor of the two-wheeled, one horse carriage with a fixed hood which became synonymous with the Victorian street scene.

SNICKETS, GINNELS, ALLEYWAYS & YARDS

The York of the Middle Ages was busy and thriving with a population of around twenty thousand, all living within the city walls. Street routes had been superimposed on the Roman roads but there was also a rabbit warren of narrow lanes which were used as short cuts.

Many of these can be explored today and comprise: snickets - passageway between walls and fences; ginnels – between or through buildings; and alleyways - providing short cuts to the market, home, church and work. These can be explored at any time as they belong to everyone and yet to nobody!

The maze of Snickelways is one of early York's intriguing legacies. The sheer number of these little thoroughfares, around fifty within the city walls, is evidence of their popularity to the foot-bound medieval resident. A high proportion of them are routed close to the sites of medieval markets, a fact illustrated by the several alleyways leading off Shambles - where the butchers traded; and from Swinegate – the former pig market. Nearby, ginnels lead off from St Sampson's Square, which was the site of York's oldest trading area known as Thursday Market.

Top of page: 'A Walk around the Snickelways of York (1983).'
Line drawing taken from Mark Jones' best selling book.

Opposite: Coffee Yard.

INTRODUCTION

GINNELS

Horn Pot Lane (linking Low Petergate and Goodramgate) takes its name from the horn making industry that used to be in this area of the city. A nearby 14th century pit, containing the remains of horns, was excavated in the 1950's.

Lund's Court (linking Swinegate and Low Petergate) was formerly known as Mad Alice Lane, a reference to Alice Smith who lived in the lane until 1825; the year she was hanged at York Castle, despite pleading insanity for the murder of her husband.

Lady Peckett's Yard (linking Pavement and Fossgate) is named after the wife of a former Lord Mayor of York.

Coffee Yard (linking Stonegate and Grape Lane) is the most intriguing and longest thoroughfare. It is extremely narrow in parts and at one point, only five foot ten inches high. It was named after York's first coffee house which opened in the area in about 1670.

St Crux Passage got its name from St Crux church which was demolished in 1887. The Snickelway links the Shambles with the shortest street in York, Whip-ma-Whop-ma-gate.

Linking Market Street with High Ousegate, Peter Lane funnels into Le Kyrk Lane, an extremely narrow passage which makes passing a very intimate process.

These eccentric little thoroughfares are still rights of way and it is possible to explore virtually the entire city centre by using this labyrinth of medieval short-cuts. Gas lamps were introduced down many ginnels in the early 19th century and later converted to electricity.

From medieval times, the ginnels have been given their own names...

Opposite: Le Kyrk Lane.

SNICKETS, GINNELS, ALLEYWAYS & YARDS

WHIP-MA-WHOP-MA-GATE

This is the shortest street with the longest name. At approximately 32 metres, it leads from Colliergate to Pavement. In the 16th century, its unusual name was Whitnourwhatnourgate which translates roughly as 'What a street! Call this a street?' Some claim that there is a darker meaning and that this street marks the site of public flogging.

…*what a street!* call this a street?

Above & opposite: Whip-ma-whop-ma-gate.

SNICKETS, GINNELS, ALLEYWAYS & YARDS

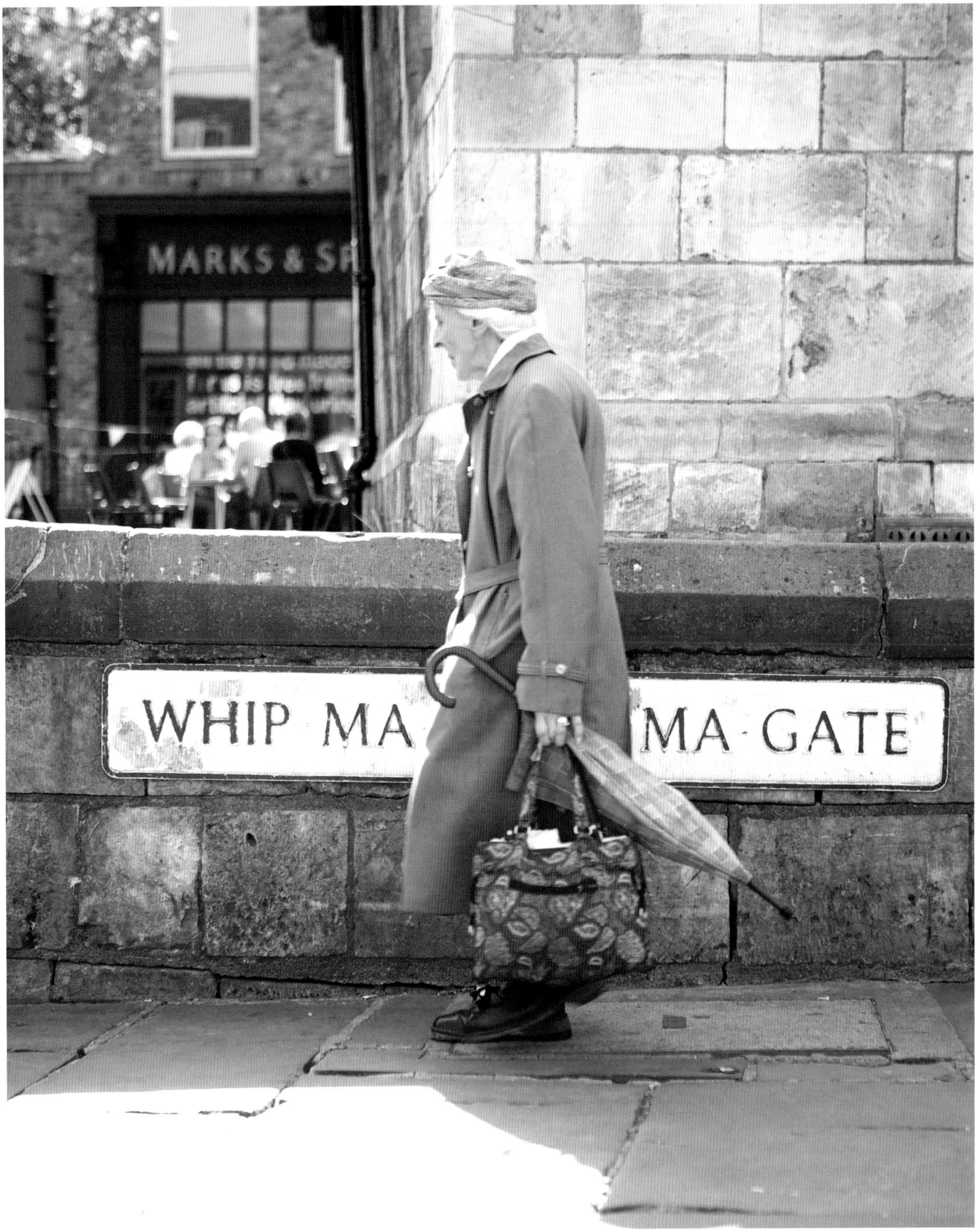

THE MINSTER

The largest Gothic cathedral north of the Alps. Even in a city full of exquisite architecture, York Minster dominates York's skyline.

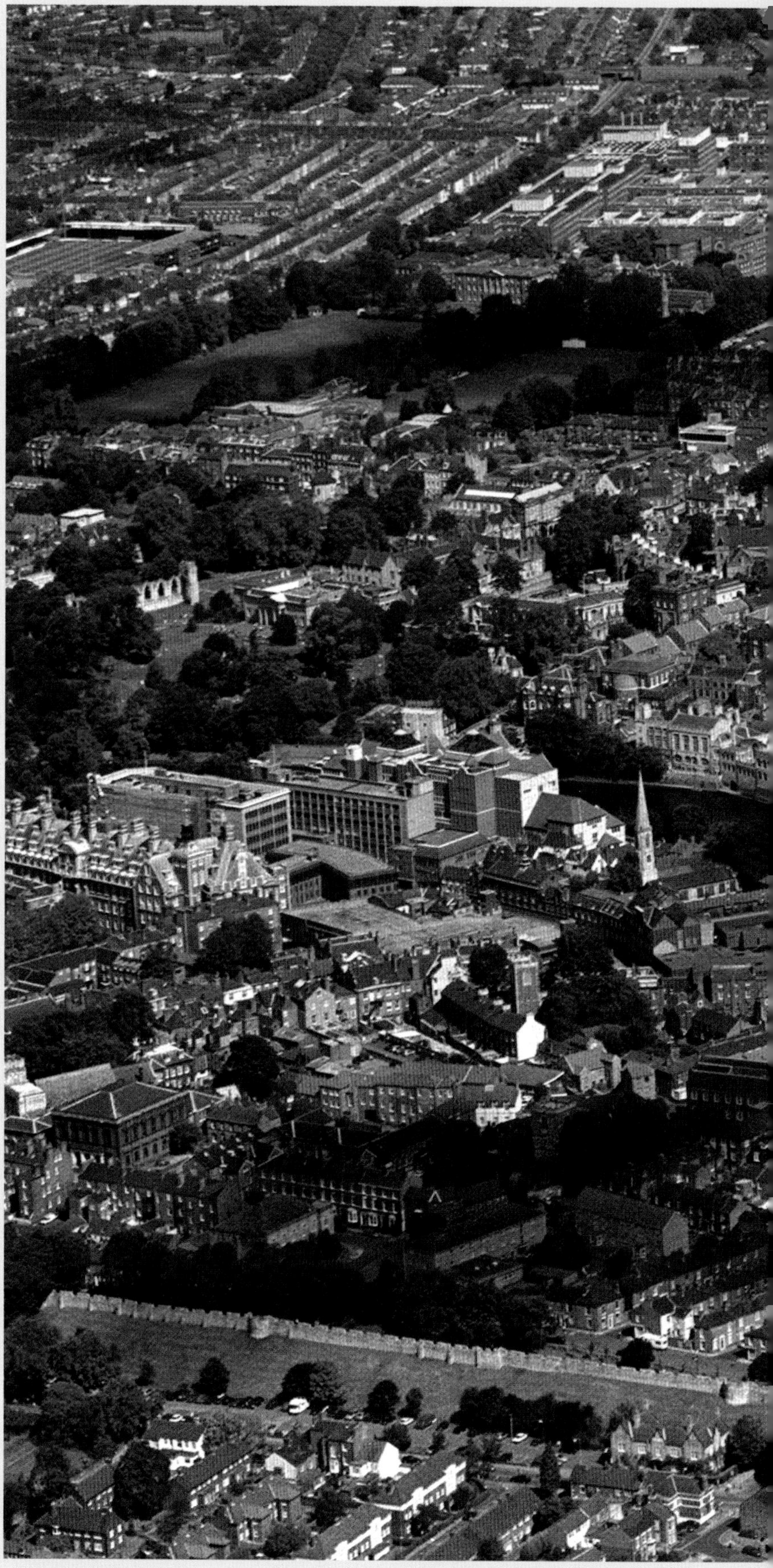

INTRODUCTION

THE MINSTER

Those visitors more accustomed to the intimate dimensions of their own parish church will be struck by the sheer size of York Minster. This is religious architecture on the very grandest of scales: over 150 metres (500ft) in length, 40 metres (130ft) wide and with a central tower almost 62 metres (200 ft) high.

This is the largest Medieval Gothic church north of the Alps and even in a city full of exquisite architecture, the Minster dominates York's skyline. Is it any wonder that visitors come from all over the world to marvel at this masterpiece - towering literally and metaphorically over the city?

As you look around the Minster, keep in mind that during the 250 years it took to complete, the only labour-saving devices were simple levers, pulleys and hoists. Its construction relied solely on manual labour and we can only guess at the number of masons and carpenters who dedicated their entire working lives to this one project.

There has been Christian worship here for more than 1,300 years and before that it was the site of the Roman Principia (the headquarters of the Roman fortress.)

The origins of the church we see today can be traced back to 1220 and a time when Archbishop Walter de Grey aspired to a cathedral that would rival Canterbury in grandeur, though there are remains of the earlier Norman cathedral, especially in the crypt.

Because its construction took a quarter of a millennium, the Minster's architecture embraces a variety of styles. The transepts are in Early English, the nave and Chapter House belong to the Decorated period and the quire and east end, which were built a little later, are of the Perpendicular style.

By 1472, with only the central tower substantially unfinished, the Minster was finally consecrated.

Today it is both a place of worship and a treasure-house of religious and architectural heritage - a place to wander and enjoy centuries of craftsmanship and devotion.

Opposite: York Minster West Door.

INTRODUCTION

INSIDE THE MINSTER

The Nave

The nave is the main body of a church and York Minster boasts the widest Gothic nave in the country. To reduce the weight of the roof, it was vaulted in wood rather than stone and scenes from the life of Christ decorate the roof bosses. Before 1863, the great nave was rarely used for church services other than processions and grand ceremonies.

The heart-shaped, curvilinear carving at the top of the Great West Window, one of many fine 14th century windows in the nave, has led to it being dubbed the 'Heart of Yorkshire' Window. Dating back to 1338, it encompasses the figures of twelve apostles and beneath them, eight Bishops and Archbishops of York.

Chapter House

This splendid octagonal building was built in the 13th century as a meeting room for the Dean and Chapter (the Minster's governing body.) The only part of the Minster to remain unconsecrated, it was adopted by Edward I as a meeting place for his parliament. The excellent acoustics lend themselves to its use as a venue for smaller concerts and musical recitals.

Architecturally, the Chapter House is a marvel, having no central support to spread the weight of the extensive vaulted ceiling. The walls are lined with canopied stalls, delicately carved with leaves, birds and human heads whose expressions range from the radiant to the grotesque.

The East End

Unlike many early Norman churches that incorporate a semi circular shape, the Minster's East end is square and dominated by the Great East Window. Glazed by John Thornton between 1405 and 1408, it is the size of a tennis court and remains the largest window of medieval glass in England. The theme of the stained glass is the beginning and end of all created things, with the figure of God represented at the top, presiding over his saints and angels.

In 2006, one of the most ambitious renovation projects of its kind was started on the East end. Scheduled to last for 10 years, it will see the replacement of crumbling stonework and the complete restoration of the window. The work is being undertaken by the Minster's own glaziers and stonemasons, the latter working with stone quarried locally near Tadcaster.

The Quire

The Quire (choir) stalls and the archbishop's throne (the cathedral) date from 1360 onwards. The throne gives the Minster its status as a cathedral – 'cathedra' being the Greek word for throne.

The quire screen was a 15th century addition and features exquisitely carved representations of fifteen kings of England – from William I to Henry VI.

Opposite: The Quire Screen.

THE MINSTER

INSIDE THE MINSTER

North Transept

The north and south transepts represent the oldest parts of the present building. In the north transept, the glass in the Five Sisters Window dates back to 1260 and is of a type known as 'grisaille'. With each stone lancet extending 53 feet high, this is the largest area of grisaille glass to have survived anywhere in the world.

If you stand at the mid-point between the north and south transepts, you can gaze up into the central tower which was completed in the late 1400s.

South Transept

Above the simple narrow windows of the south transept is the exquisite Rose Window. It was this part of the Minster that suffered the most damage during the fire of 1984. The roof was all but destroyed and the glass in the Rose Window shattered into thousands of pieces. Fortunately, because the leading had recently been restored, no glass was lost and the restoration of the Window entrusted to the craftsmen of the Glaziers Trust who look after all the Minster's stained glass.

The tomb of Archbishop Walter de Grey, (it was he who began the rebuilding of the old Norman church) rests here in the south transept and is thought to be the finest of the Minster's many monuments.

The Aisles

Tombs and plaques commemorate many notable figures from the past – some religious, some secular. Surprisingly, there is only one royal tomb: that of Prince William of Hatfield who died as an infant in 1346. His recumbent effigy lies in a canopied niche in the wall of the north quire aisle.

Many other monuments line the aisles and side-chapels, and in the Zouche Chapel can be found the only 15th century quire stalls to have survived the fire of 1829.

Left: The Rose Window

Opposite: Five Sisters Window.

THE MINSTER

THE CRYPT

Reached from the south quire aisle, the crypt is revealed as the earliest part of the Minster to be built. It contains remains of the crypt as rebuilt in the 12th century as well as a 14th century font.

Recent explorations, during work to the fabric of the building, revealed details of the Minster's earliest years. By exploring the undercroft, visitors can literally walk through the Minster's history.

Foundations

When building work began in the 13th century, huge quantities of stone were quarried near Tadcaster and transported to York via the Rivers Wharfe and Ouse. This magnesian limestone, almost white when first quarried, weathers in time to the attractive honey-coloured hue we see today.

A building of such age, importance and size presents monumental problems with its upkeep and it became apparent by the 1960s that without a massive programme of restoration, the Minster would not be around for much longer. The crisis prompted a successful appeal for funds and though services were never interrupted, between 1967 and 1972 the interior of the Minster resembled a building site more than a place of worship.

By getting, literally, to the bottom of the problem, engineers realised that some of the medieval foundations had to be consolidated or even replaced. Hydraulic jacks were used to raise buckling foundations before concrete 'girdles' could reinforce them. It was, in its own way, as monumental a task as some of the original building work but it provided archaeologists with the opportunity to investigate the site's 2,000-year history.

What they found surpassed all expectations. The foundations of the Norman Minster were unearthed, as well as important relics from other periods including an Anglo Saxon graveyard and a Roman culvert that still helps to divert water away from the foundations.

Opposite: Anglo Saxon Gravestone.
Copyright Dean and Chapter of York.

THE MINSTER

FIRE, FIRE!

Over the centuries, the Minster has had its fair share of fires, three of which occurred during more recent times.

In 1829, Jonathan Martin, a deranged religious zealot was convinced that he had been sent by God to destroy the Minster. He made a pile of hymn-books in the quire and set them alight before escaping. While his effort to destroy the Minster failed, it resulted in the setting up of the Minster police, who still guard the building both day and night. Martin was apprehended and ended his days in a mental asylum.

Just eleven years later another fire – this time a tragic accident caused by a candle – gave rise to serious damage to the west end. Troops were called out, but more to calm the swelling crowds of people than to douse the flames. Fire engines, requisitioned from Leeds and Tadcaster, were brought to York via the recently completed railway.

The most recent fire in July 1984 saw flames from the South Transept light up the night sky. It was thought that an electrical storm was the most likely cause, though the consecration, a few weeks previously, of a controversial bishop caused some people to wonder whether there might have been divine intervention!

Above & opposite: The fire of 1984 lit up the night sky.

THE MINSTER

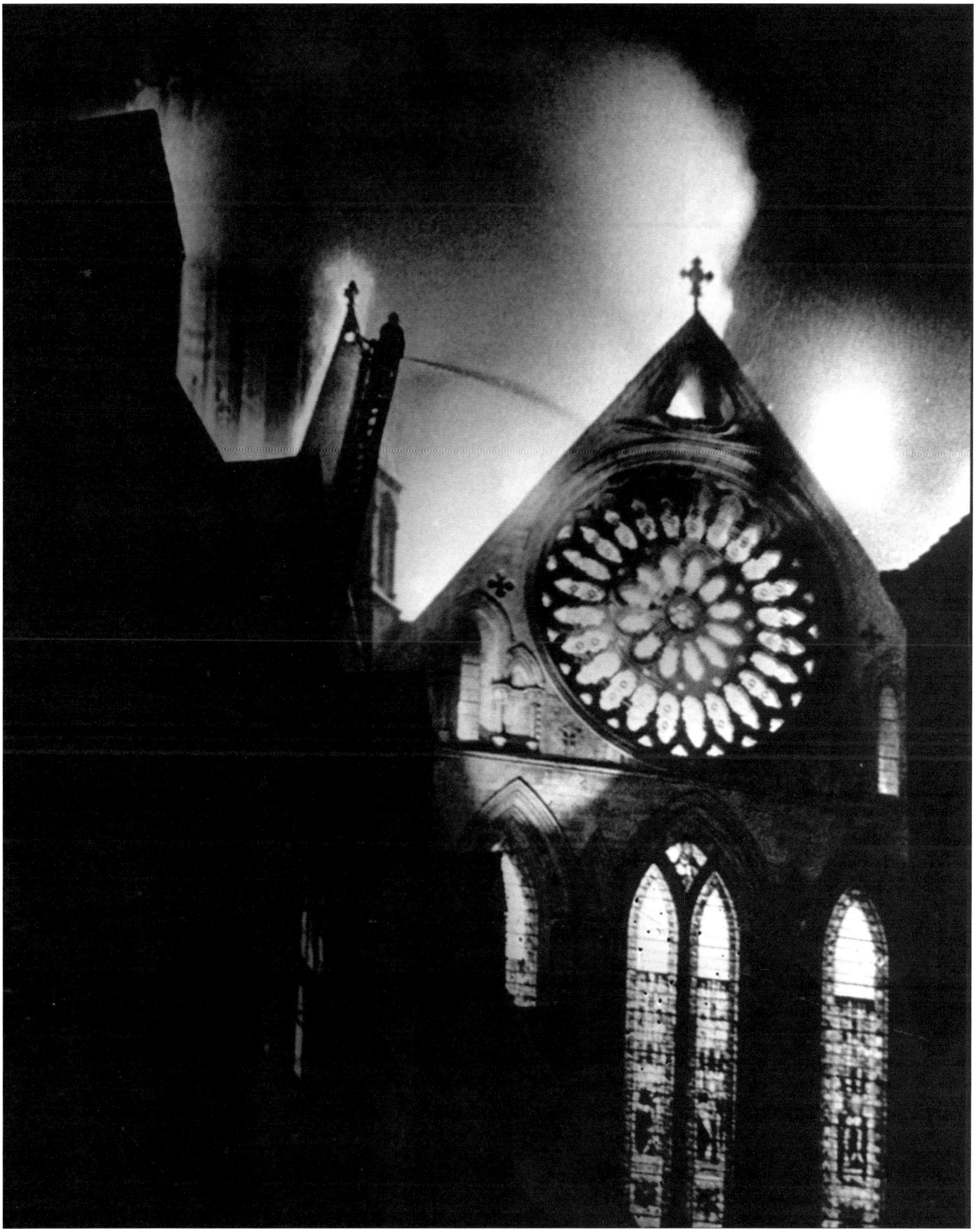

WALK THE MINSTER PRECINCT

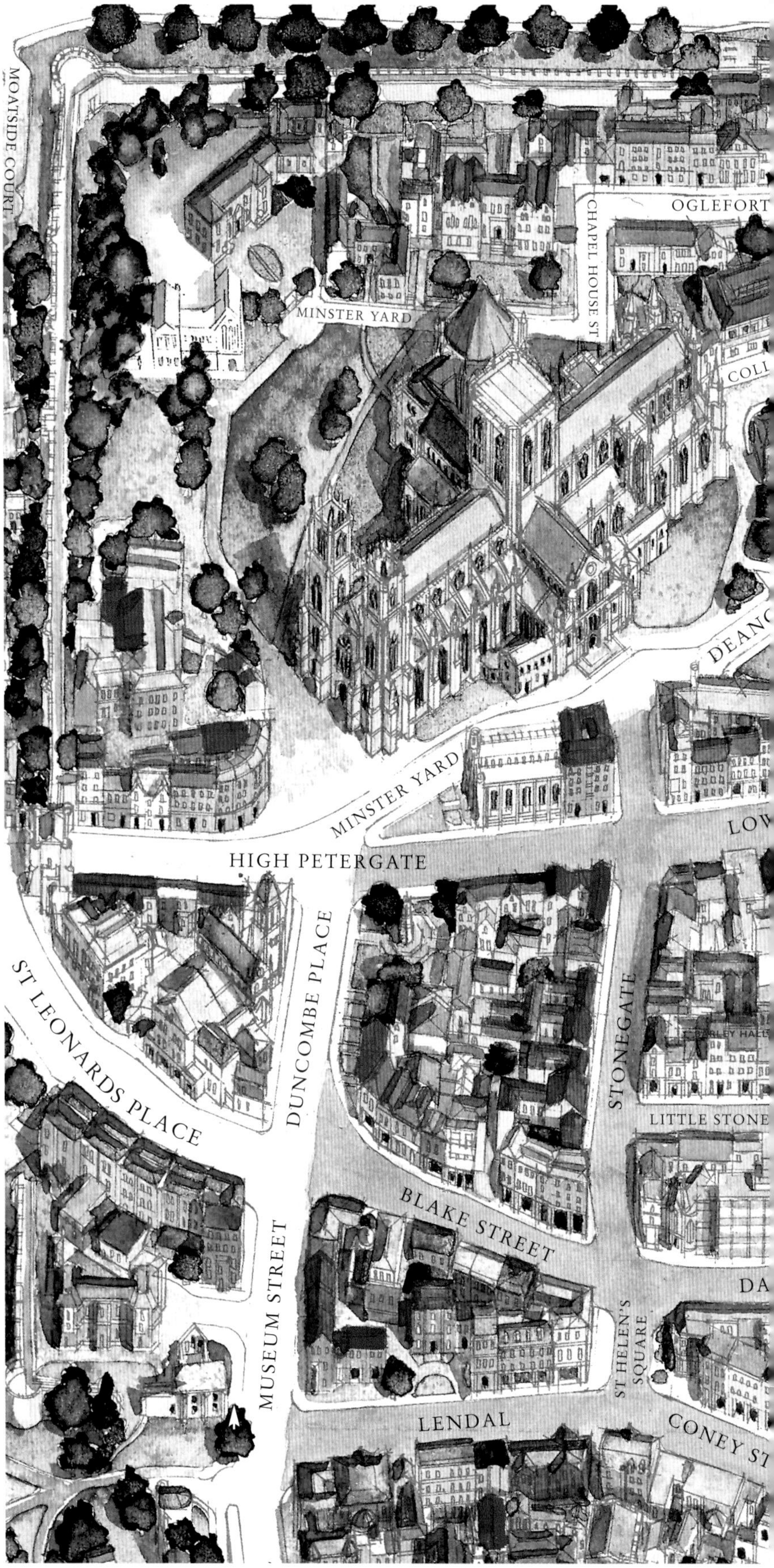

Having explored the wonders of the Minster, cast your eyes a little wider and discover some of its neighbouring streets and buildings.

Throughout the Middle Ages, the area immediately around the Minster was enclosed within its own wall and was known as the Liberty of St Peter. Four gateways gave access to this 'close', one of which (the overhanging portion of the National Trust shop) survives.

Stand by the steps at the door to the South Transept - now the main entrance to the Minster. Above you is the Rose Window and in front, across the road stands a fourth century Roman column. Originally one of sixteen supporting the Great Hall of the Roman Principia (the central building of the Roman fortress) which was occupied by the Sixth Legion, it was found buried in 1969 during excavations for repairs to the Minster's central tower. The Dean and Chapter (the Minster's governing body) gave the column to York Civic Trust who erected it in 1971 to mark the 1900th year of the city's foundation. Some say it is upside down, which causes amusement, but this is strongly denied!

To the left of the steps is the impressive statue of the Roman Emperor, Constantine the Great (AD 274-337).

INTRODUCTION

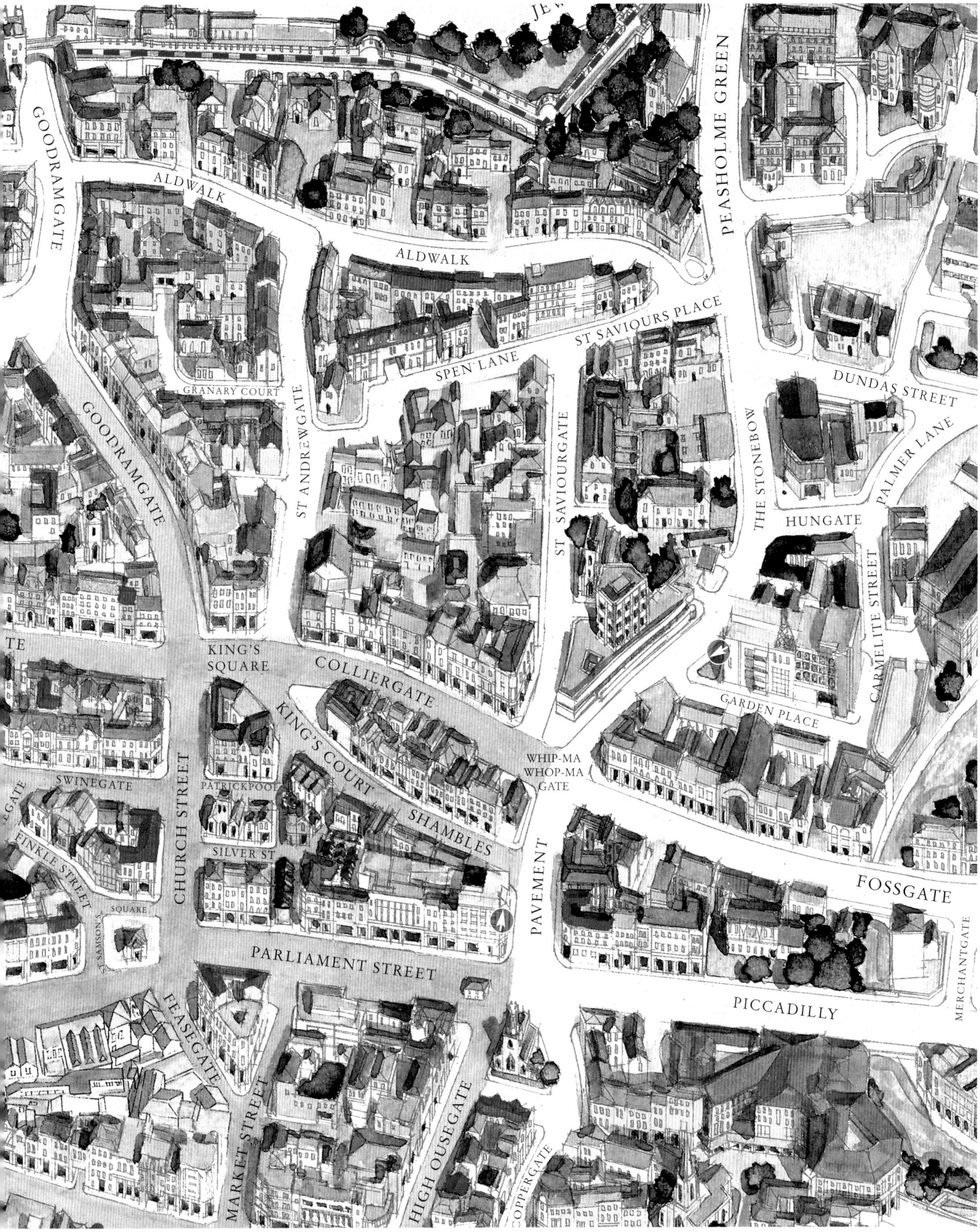

CONSTANTINE

A *message* from god

It is said that Constantine's conversion to Christianity came as a result of a vision he had on the eve of the battle of Milvian Bridge near Rome. A cross appeared over the sun and he heard a voice cry: "In this sign conquer". He then ordered his troops to scratch the sign of the cross on their shields in order to ensure victory.

Continue along Deangate with the Minster on your left. Across the road is the Minster School, an independent preparatory school which was built in 1833. Known originally as St Peter's School, it became the Minster Song School in 1903. It is no longer necessary to be a chorister to attend, but it is still the school where the boys (and more recently girls) who sing in the Minster choir are educated. The choristers' days are long with many rehearsals. During late afternoons, they can be heard singing Evensong in the Minster's Quire.

Just past the school, peep through the double gates on the right. This is the entrance to the Minster Stoneyard, which is occasionally open to the public. Here the magnesian limestone, quarried near Tadcaster, is prepared for use in constant restoration work.

At the East End of the Minster, one of the largest restoration programmes of its kind began in 2006 to repair the famous Great East Window and crumbling stonework. This project will take many years to complete.

Above: Stained glass in the Minster's East Window.

Opposite: Constantine the Great.

WALK THE MINSTER PRECINCT

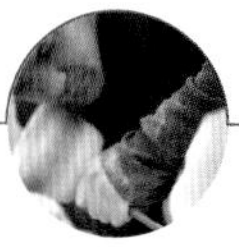

RESTORATION

In front of the window, just to the right across the cobbles, is St. William's College. This black and white timbered building was founded in 1461 on the orders of Edward IV, as a home for the Minster Chantry Priests (whose main task was to say mass for the souls of deceased benefactors.) This practice was stopped during the Reformation, and since then the building has been used as a townhouse, printing press and assorted shops. Today the college provides a tranquil setting for a restaurant and conference centre.

Beyond the College and closer to the Minster, there is some medieval (and later) housing, before you reach Chapter House Street which follows the line of the Via Decumana – the Roman street leading to the north east gate of the fortress.

Cross the end of Chapter House Street. To your left is the Chapter House itself and to your right, the splendid Treasurer's House. Originally the home of the Canon Treasurer, it became Crown property during the Reformation. Then it had a variety of tenants until it was acquired by the National Trust following a major restoration in 1930. Today the house is open to the public and provides the setting for one of York's most famous ghost stories!

Enter Dean's Park through the gate on your left. This was the site of the original Archbishop's palace: the fragmentary remains of a cloister can be seen across the grass and, to its right, the chapel which now houses part of the Minster Library. This is the largest Cathedral library in England and is open to the public. As the "Old" palace declined in favour of the "New" one at Bishopthorpe, some of its materials were re-used to build a large mansion for the Ingram family. This was finally demolished in 1792. At the west end of the park is the old Purey Cust hospital. Converted and extended from Canons' housing in 1915, it was named after Dean Purey-Cust who died in 1916. His grave may be seen in front of the Five Sisters Window, and is the only one outside the Minster. The park also contained St Sepulchre's Chapel (which connected with the Minster) and the Peter Prison. Neither of these survive.

As you leave the park through the gates turn left past the West Front of the Minster. The church of St Michael - le- Belfrey stands to your right. This was the last parish church in York to be completed before the Reformation, and the only one to be built entirely in the "perpendicular" phase of the Gothic style. This is where Guy Fawkes was baptised in 1570, and the Minster is actually in its parish! Note that St Michael's is not parallel with the Minster, but orientated at about 45 degrees to it. It appears to be aligned with the underlying Roman street plan and this might indicate that one of its predecessors may have had a very early origin indeed! Pass between St Michael's and the Minster to return to the South Transept steps below the Rose Window.

Left: Stained glass in the Minster's East Window.

Opposite: Minster stonemasons at work.

WALK THE MINSTER PRECINCT

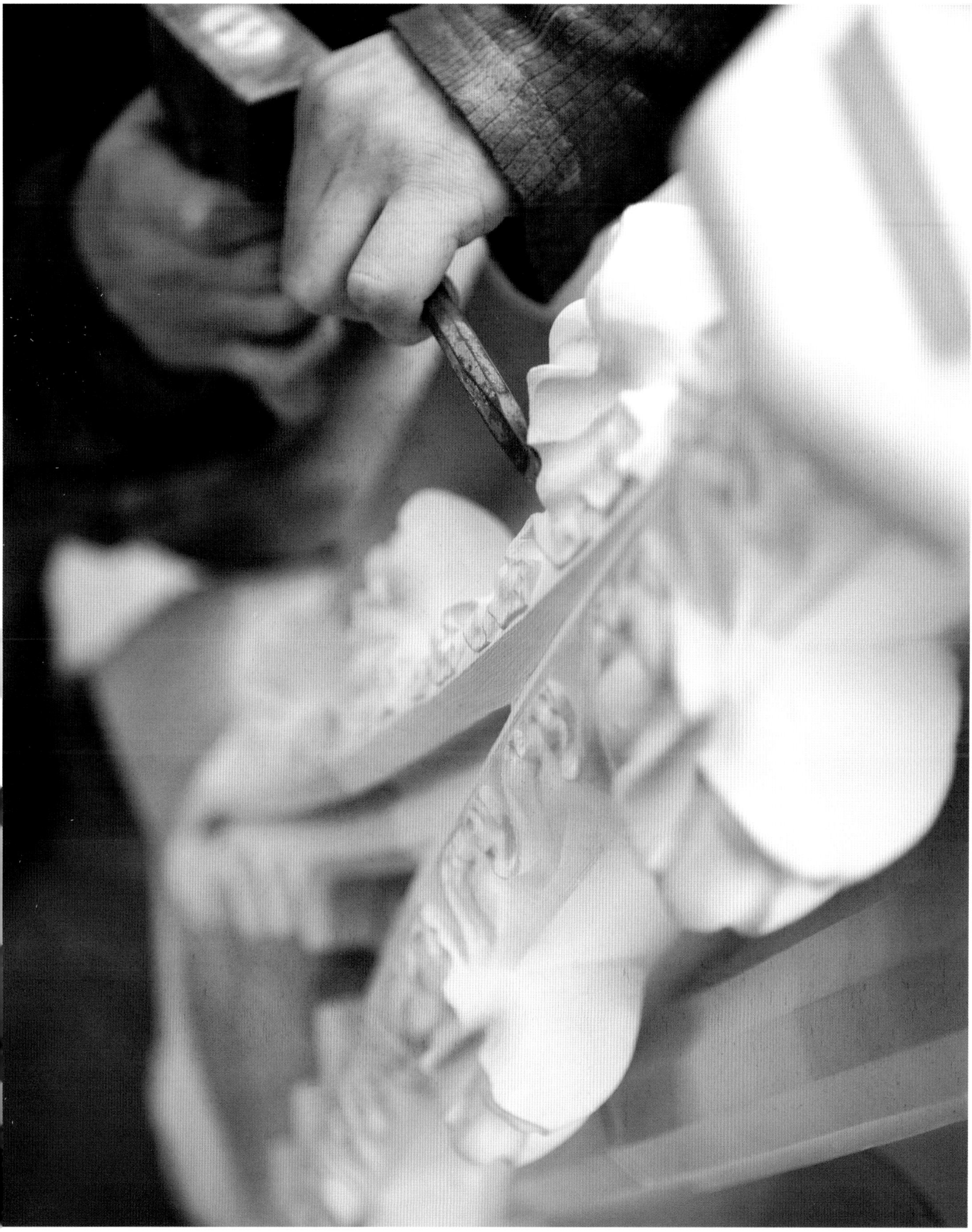

07

HISTORIC BUILDINGS

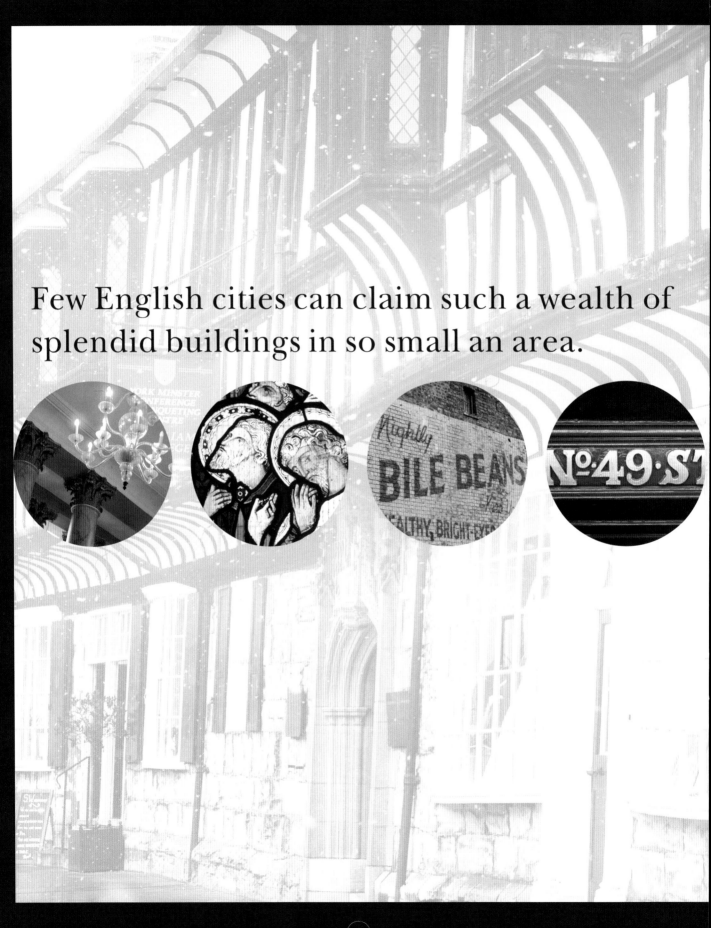

Few English cities can claim such a wealth of splendid buildings in so small an area.

INTRODUCTION

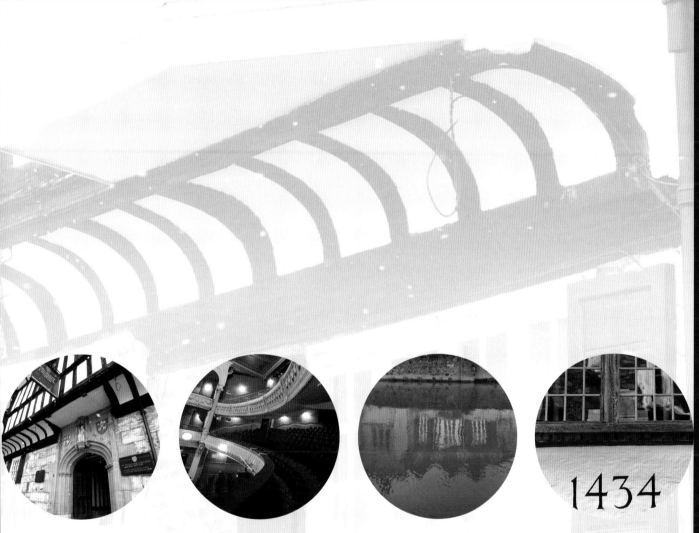

Take time to discover each and enjoy a diverse assortment of architecture, unique settings and interiors.

ASSEMBLY ROOMS

Built between 1730 and 1735 and designed by Richard Boyle, 3rd Earl of Burlington, York's Assembly Rooms are probably Europe's earliest example of neo-classical architecture. The elegant interior is of a style copied from the Italian architect Palladio's Egyptian Hall and displays a ceiling supported by 48 massive Corinthian columns.

The building was a fashionable meeting place for the local gentry in the 18th century and provided a setting for winter entertainment. This usually consisted of card games and dancing but the rooms eventually became associated with York Races as a stylish place to meet before and after race meetings.

As time went by, assemblies became less popular and over the next 200 years the rooms were only used occasionally for dancing and concerts. In 2002 the Assembly Rooms were purchased by the York Conservation Trust and today, with their new role as a popular restaurant, can easily be visited and enjoyed.

Above & opposite: Assembly Rooms, Blake Street.

HISTORIC BUILDINGS

BARLEY HALL & BEDERN HALL

Barley Hall

Built on a site once occupied by a monastic hostel, this 14th century timber frame house was home to William Snawsell, a goldsmith who was also Lord Mayor and friend of Richard III. Recently restored and tucked away in Coffee Yard, (just off Stonegate), it is well worth discovering. A giant window enables passers-by to view the dining room from the outside – even after the house is closed.

Bedern Hall

Derived from the Anglo-Saxon meaning 'house of prayer', Bedern was a small area comprising the college of the Vicars Choral, their housing, a dining hall and chapel. These vicars were priests who were paid to sing services in the Minster. Records show that when it was founded in 1349, there were 36 Vicars Choral living in Bedern.

One interesting feature associated with the hall but no longer visible, was a bridge which linked the college area with Minster Close on the far side of Goodramgate. This enabled the vicars to travel between the two places but avoid contact with 'common folk'.

The present hall was built around 1370 as a shared dining area for the priests up to the time of the Reformation. It continued to be used for meetings and feasts but its upkeep was difficult and by 1650, part of it was incorporated into a private house.

During the late 18th century, the Hall was divided into tenements and by the 1840s had deteriorated into a slum with a mainly Irish population. It was described as a "sad spectacle of poverty and wretchedness".

The Bedern National School was built in the area in the 1870s and since then the hall has been used as a bakery and pork pie factory. In 1971, most of the buildings were demolished and the hall and chapel restored. The Guilds of Freemen, Master Builders and The Company of Cordwainers (workers in fine leather) adopted Bedern as their guild hall and today it is available for private hire.

Above: Barley Hall. Opposite: Bedern Hall.

HISTORIC BUILDINGS

BISHOPTHORPE PALACE

Bishopthorpe Palace

For almost 800 years, the Archbishops of York have enjoyed this stunning riverside setting as their official residence.

Situated just two miles north west of the city, the village of Bishopthorpe was so named when Archbishop Walter De Grey bought the village of Thorpe St Andrew in 1241. Here he built a country residence and chapel, some of which remains today, and over time the village became known as Bishopthorpe. The palace has endured some turbulent history, falling into disrepair and being sold to a Parliamentarian for £567. At the restoration of the Monarchy, the newly appointed Archbishop renovated the Great Hall. The present façade and gatehouse date from the 1760's.

The palace was home to the only Archbishop of York to be executed. Archbishop Richard Scrope was brought before the king and found guilty of treason. He was beheaded in Clementhorpe in 1405 but was looked upon as a martyr and his tomb in York Minster became a place of pilgrimage.

Top of page: Archbishop of York, Dr John Sentamu.

Opposite: Bishopthorpe Palace, 2 miles downstream from the city.

HISTORIC BUILDINGS

CLIFFORD'S TOWER

Rising dramatically from its steep, grassy mound, Clifford's Tower is one of the city's most familiar landmarks. Originally one of two wooden castles built by William the Conqueror as part of his northern military headquarters, it witnessed one of York's most infamous events. In 1190, when threatened by an angry mob, the city's Jewish people sought sanctuary here. Faced with the prospect of enforced baptism or death, they chose instead to commit mass suicide. The pursuing mob turned their anger on the castle and burned it to the ground along with the bodies of York's Jewish community.

During Henry III's reign, the tower was rebuilt in stone as the keep to a substantial fortification - made even more secure by a moat that was fed by diverting the River Foss. Following the Battle of Boroughbridge in 1322, the defeated Roger de Clifford was hung in chains from its battlements and the tower was named after him.

Over the centuries, Clifford's Tower has had numerous uses; first as York's administrative centre, then as a prison. By Victorian times, it formed part of a large prison complex which included the buildings that now comprise the Castle Museum. In more recent years the uglier prison buildings were demolished and Clifford's Tower was opened up once again to the public. It is now in the care of English Heritage.

Above & opposite: Clifford's Tower

HISTORIC BUILDINGS

FAIRFAX HOUSE & GUILDHALL

Fairfax House, *Castlegate*

The finest of Georgian residences, Fairfax House was completed in 1762 for the ninth Viscount Fairfax as a dowry for his only surviving child Anne Fairfax. At that time, the city was at the height of its popularity amongst the leisured classes and many wealthy families came to York to enjoy its culture and ambience. Over the years the house's fortunes declined and many spectacular features were lost behind plaster-board to make way for 20th century demand and its use as both a cinema and nightclub. It was rescued from further damage in 1982 by York Civic Trust and, following an imaginative restoration programme, was brought back to its former life by filling the rooms with items of period furniture previously owned by Noel Terry, the famous confectioner.

Guildhall, *St Helen's Square*

Traditionally the city's administrative centre, the medieval Guildhall is a reminder of the power and influence once enjoyed by York's craft guilds. They effectively controlled the trade in the city and looked after their members' interests.

The present building, which stands hidden behind the Mansion House and is best viewed from the river, dates from the 15th century and occupies the site where the Romans built the first Ouse bridge. It suffered serious bomb damage in 1942 but was rebuilt to its original design. Inside, the roof of the main hall is supported by two rows of huge oak columns – each made from a single length of wood. An adjoining room – the inner chamber – is the one part of the building to have survived the bombers.

Above: Fairfax House. Opposite: The Guildhall.

HISTORIC BUILDINGS

GRAND OPERA HOUSE & CITY SCREEN

Grand Opera House

Originally built in 1868 as a Corn Exchange, the building was converted to a theatre by William Peacock in the early 1900's. Varied programmes attracted large audiences and numerous stars of the day trod its boards including Charlie Chaplin, Gracie Fields, Lillie Langtry, Cicely Courtneidge and Jimmy Jewel. In 1945, new owners introduced a raft of personalities such as Vera Lynn, Laurel and Hardy and Morecombe and Wise but sadly, live theatre was unable to compete with the popularity of television and audiences dwindled. To keep up with the demands of post war Britain, much of the interior was removed and replaced with a flat floor suitable for roller skating, dancing, bingo and wrestling until finally closing its doors in 1985.

A £4 million investment by new owners restored the building to a theatre and a second renovation in 2002 has ensured that the curtain continues to rise on a variety of shows from classical plays and West End musicals to opera, ballet and comedy.

City Screen

This award winning cinema in Coney Street opened in 2000 as part of a redevelopment project incorporating the former Yorkshire Herald building, the façade of which fronts the River Ouse. The cinema is famous for showing more obscure and less advertised films as well the popular.

Above & opposite: The Grand Opera House's splendid auditorium.

HISTORIC BUILDINGS

KING'S MANOR

The royal coat of arms displayed prominently over the main door is that of King Charles I.

HISTORIC BUILDINGS

King's Manor, *Exhibition Square*

First built around 1270, and rebuilt in brick in 1490, as the residence of the abbot of St Mary's Abbey, this medieval building has endured a chequered history. Following the dissolution of the monasteries, it fell into royal ownership and became known as King's Manor. As a royal residence, many monarchs stayed here including Henry VIII, James VI of Scotland (later to become James I of England) and the court of Charles I. The Council of the North was established here by Charles I, making York effectively the 'capital' of the North of England. During the Civil War, the council was disbanded and the building became the Royalist headquarters. Over the next 300 years, King's Manor suffered a similar fate to other fine York buildings and served a variety of purposes including apartments, gaming rooms, a girls' boarding school and the Yorkshire School for the Blind until finally, during the 1960s, it was taken over by York University.

Despite being altered and extended many times, the peaceful courtyards, gabled roofs, decorative doorways and imaginative brickwork make this is one of the city's most evocative buildings.

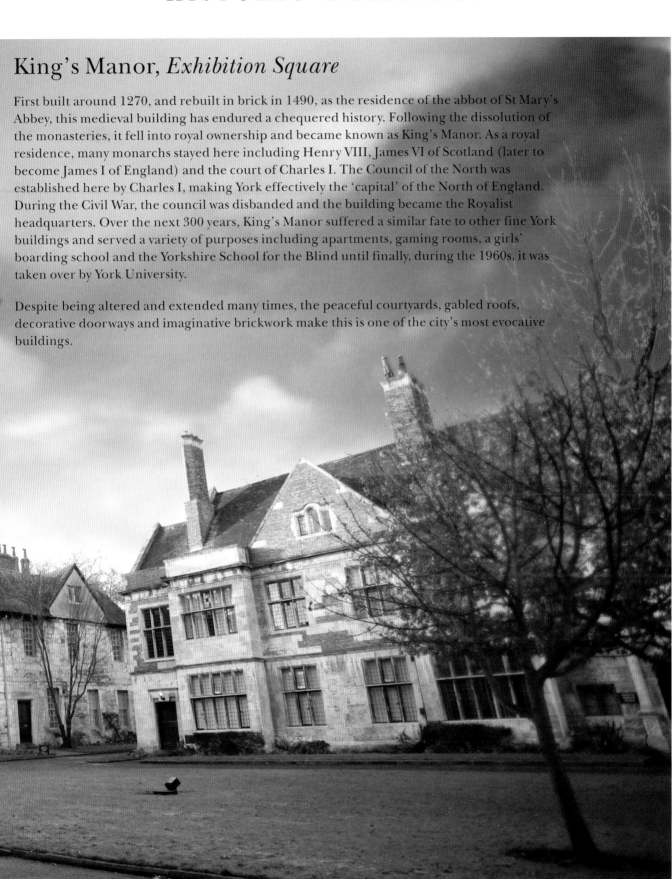

MERCHANT ADVENTURERS' HALL

Merchant Adventurers' Hall, *Fossgate*

Completed in 1362, this outstanding building remains one of the best preserved medieval guild halls in the country. The Merchant Adventurers were the most important of the many craft guilds in the city and for centuries had a monopoly over the sale of imported and exported goods – particularly cloth. No shop could be opened in the city without their permission and its importance is reflected in the hall's stature, being the largest timber-framed building in the city. The hall remains today largely unchanged, apart from periodic refurbishments. Records kept show a remarkable account of all the materials used in its construction including 100 trees. The Undercroft, with its adjoining chapel, was used as a hospital while upstairs, the Great Hall has an undulating wooden floor and splendid open-timbered roof.

Top of page & opposite: Merchant Adventurers' Hall

Bottom of page opposite: Stained Glass panel in Governor's parlour.

HISTORIC BUILDINGS

MANSION HOUSE, MERCHANT TAYLORS & BATHS

Mansion House

This elegant townhouse still remains the official residence of the Lord Mayor during his or her year of office. It was built between 1725 and 1730 by a committee of Aldermen. The house is home to an impressive collection of civic regalia ranging from paintings and furniture to medieval ceremonial swords and a solid silver chamber pot! Restored by York Civic Trust in 1999, the Mansion House is open to the public for guided tours on Fridays and Saturdays between March and Christmas.

Merchant Taylors' Hall

This guild hall originally belonged to the Fraternity of St John the Baptist and dates from around 1400. As one of the few surviving halls, it was used originally for the drapers, hosiers and tailors, becoming the Merchant Taylors in 1662. The brick exterior dates from the late seventeenth century and two well preserved stained glass windows by Henry Gyles depict the coats of arms of the Guild as well as a portrait of Queen Anne. The Hall is not usually open to the public but is a popular venue for weddings and banquets.

The Roman Bath, *St Sampson's Square*

This museum is in the basement of a public house which has been built on the site of the original Roman Bathhouse. Excavated during the 1930s, drinkers had long been able to take a peek at the remains through a glass panel in the floor.

Now the baths have been opened up to the public and from a walkway visitors can examine parts of the baths where the soldiers of the Ninth Legion would keep themselves clean. (See p.14)

Above: Solid silver chamber pot, part of impressive collection of Mansion House silver.

Coat of Arms above the door to the Merchant Taylors' Hall

Roman Bath Public House.

Opposite: The Mansion House still remains home to the City's Lord Mayor.

HISTORIC BUILDINGS

ST MARY'S ABBEY

St Mary's Abbey, *Museum Gardens*

Stand and reflect on the enchanting 13th century ruins of St Mary's Abbey and it's not hard to imagine the monastic buildings as they would have been. A mill, granary and brew-house would all have been incorporated as part of a self-sufficient way of life. The abbey was the second to be built here, the first pre-dating it by 200 years and built on land donated by William II.

The Benedictine monks created one of the wealthiest communities in the north and because the abbey was just outside the city walls, it was given its own perimeter wall and, in the 14th century, reinforced with battlements.

Henry VIII brought the abbey's prosperity to an abrupt end in 1539 and much of its stone was recycled for new building projects. All that survives today are a few evocative ruins in a tranquil garden setting which have occasionally been used as a backdrop to the York Mystery Plays.

Above: York Mystery Plays. *Courtesy National Centre for Early Music.*

Opposite: Visitors enjoy the serenity of St Mary's Abbey.

HISTORIC BUILDINGS

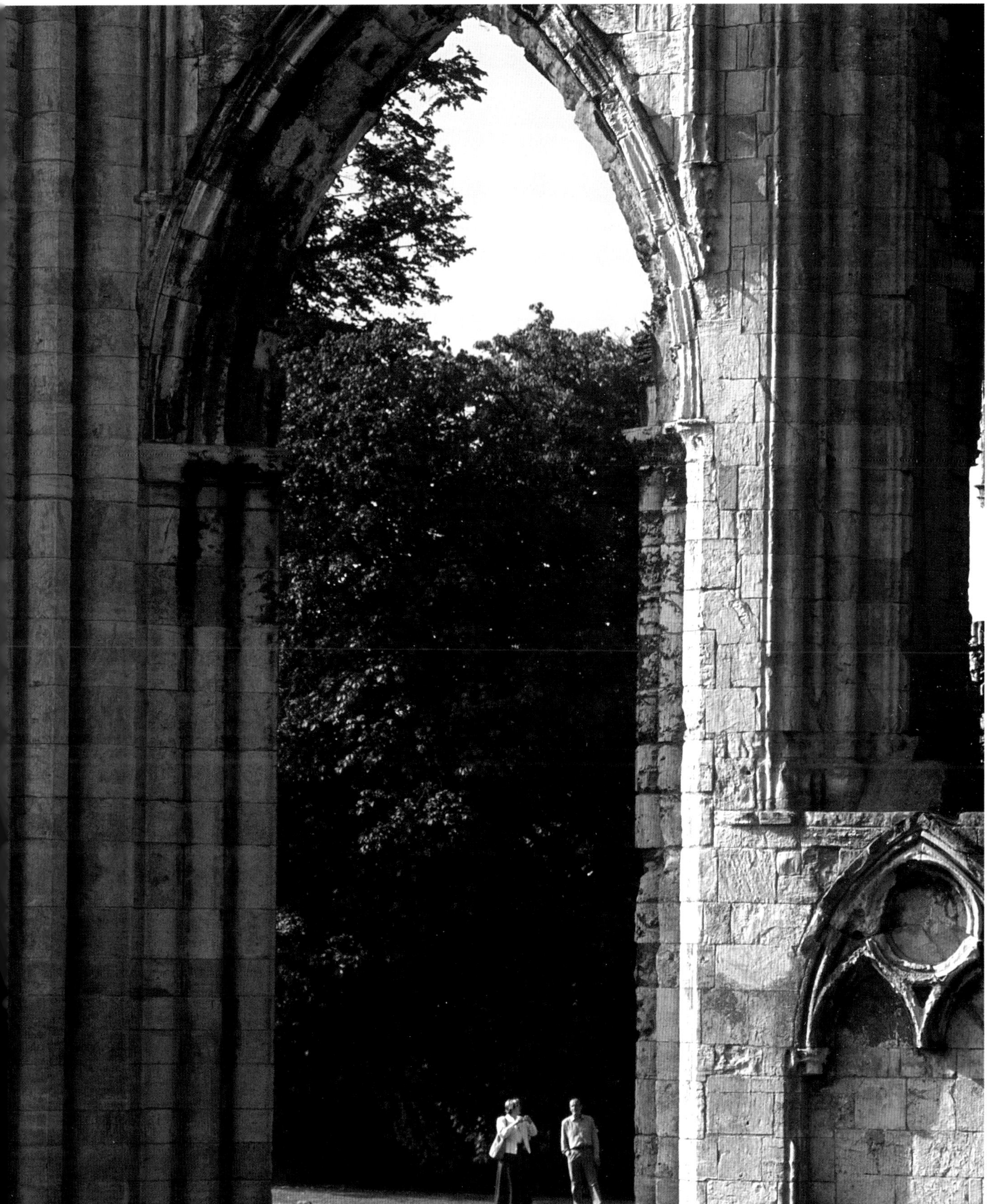

ST WILLIAM'S COLLEGE

St William's College

The duties of the Minster Chantry priests in the 15th century were undemanding. These young men, over-paid and under-employed, gained a reputation for boisterousness...and worse.

St William's College was built around 1461 to house and keep them out of trouble. Dedicated to William Fitzherbert who had been Archbishop of York 300 years earlier, the building provided accommodation for twenty three priests and a provost to oversee them.

HISTORIC BUILDINGS

ollowing the Reformation, the college was put to a variety of uses from private esidence to squalid tenements. When Charles I ruled from York it housed the royal rinting press and, as such, it is quite a miracle that this handsome, half-timbered uilding has survived relatively unscathed, to the present day.

he main doors are modern and the work of Robert Thompson of Kilburn, whose rademark, a carved mouse, appears on the right-hand door. Step through here into a ourtyard where, in summer, visitors can enjoy a meal served from the adjoining estaurant. More in keeping with its original purpose, the building itself now serves as he Minster's Visitor Centre and some of the medieval rooms are open to the public.

TREASURER'S HOUSE

Treasurer's House, *Minster Yard*

The fine building we see today was built as a private residence at the end of the 16th century and replaced a much older property. Its origin can be traced back nearly 1000 years to a time when York's first Norman Archbishop, Thomas of Bayeux discovered the Minster's affairs to be in disarray. He created the post of treasurer with the responsibility to manage the Minster – even matters as mundane as keeping the altars supplied with candles and overseeing repairs. This remained an important role, at least until Henry VIII disbanded the monasteries and appropriated the Minster's treasures.

Like so many of York's finest buildings, Treasurer's House fell into disrepair during the last century, only to be rescued by Frank Green, a wealthy local businessman. Not content with just renovating the house, he left it, together with an outstanding collection of antiques, to the National Trust.

Today, visitors can explore its magnificent interior, admire the artful blending of many architectural styles and learn about the site's convoluted history.... and its ghosts!

HISTORIC BUILDINGS

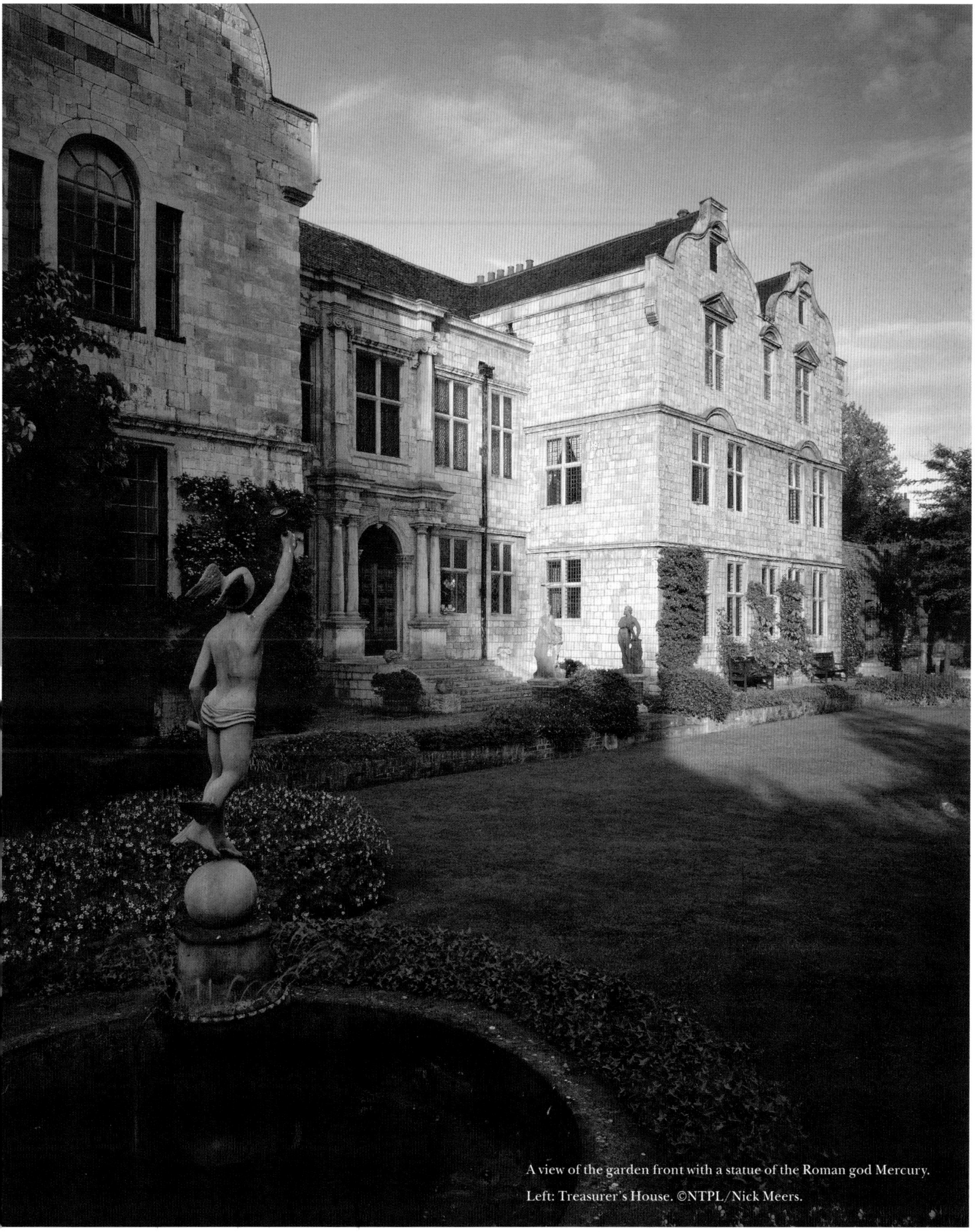

A view of the garden front with a statue of the Roman god Mercury.

Left: Treasurer's House. ©NTPL/Nick Meers.

RACECOURSE & THEATRE ROYAL

York Racecourse

Race meetings have been held in York on the Knavesmire since 1731, though race goers had to wait 20 years before enjoying the luxury of a purpose built stand. This paved the way for York to become one of the UK's most prestigious flat racing courses and in 2001, was voted 'Racecourse of the Year' by the Racegoers' Club and the Racehorse Owners' Club.

In 2005, when the course at Ascot was closed for reconstruction, York hosted the five day Royal Ascot meet in the presence of the Queen and the Royal Family. The 18 days of racing hosted by York Racecourse each year provide an exceptionally memorable day out.

York Theatre Royal

Few people appreciate that until being granted its Royal licence in 1769, the Theatre Royal was illegal. This put Thomas Keregan in breach of the law when, in 1734, he founded his theatre company in a converted tennis court in Minster Yard. After his death some 10 years later, his wife continued to flout the law and built York's New Theatre in the yard of the city's Mint. The Mint itself had been built amongst the ruins of the old St. Leonard's Hospital, one of the largest medieval hospitals in England.

Even today there remains a 16th century gateway at the back of the stage which was cut into the boundary wall to allow access to the Mint. Renamed in 1769 to mark its legalisation, the historical elegance of the auditorium contrasts well with the modern architecture of the café area and the newly built Studio space.

Above: Berwick Kaler plays the Dame in the infamous York Theatre Royal pantomime.

Opposite: York is one of the finest racecourses in the country.

HISTORIC BUILDINGS & VENUES

RIVER OUSE, BRIDGES & TOWERS

The River Ouse and its smaller tributary, the Foss, flow through the heart of York providing a natural playground for sightseers, pleasure boats and rowers. All this is in sharp contrast to a time when these waterways played a crucial role in the city's industrial growth.

Roman galleys and Viking longships reached the Ouse via the Humber Estuary.
When the Romans originally surveyed the area for building a settlement, they chose the confluence of the two rivers where a slight ridge in the otherwise flat landscape offered protection from flooding. It was from this site that Roman Eboracum, then Viking Jorvik and finally the modern city of York was able to develop into a major port and trading centre.

York's bridges

Five bridges span the Ouse in York: three carry road traffic, one trains and the most recent is used by foot passengers and cyclists.
The first bridge to be built was by the Romans, outside the main gate of their fort, at a point near where the Guildhall is today. The later Ouse Bridge began as a wooden structure which collapsed into the river beneath the weight of a crowd that congregated in 1154 to welcome Archbishop William to the city. Amazingly, no lives were lost. Old engravings depict a 14th century stone bridge, lined with shops along its full length but when this too collapsed – causing five fatalities – it was rebuilt with a larger stone arch. Ouse Bridge remained the only way of crossing the river, apart from ferry boats, until the mid 19th century.

The coming of the railways led to the construction in 1845 of the Scarborough Railway Bridge. A footpath ran between the two train lines to allow people to cross the river but in 1875, the track was re laid 4 feet above the footpath level and the path was moved to the south side of the bridge.

Constructed of cast iron, Lendal Bridge was designed to provide better access to the city from the railway station, which at that time was located within the city walls. The first structure collapsed spectacularly with reverberations being felt many miles away. Its replacement was the elegant iron bridge in place today and was designed by Thomas Page, better known for London's Westminster Bridge. The project was backed by George Hudson and in 1863 despite delays, financial squabbles and opposition from the Leeman family and local ferry owners, the engineers and labourers enjoyed a sit-down dinner on the bridge to celebrate its opening. Tolls were subsequently collected from the small building on the bridge where, at one time, there had been a rope ferry.

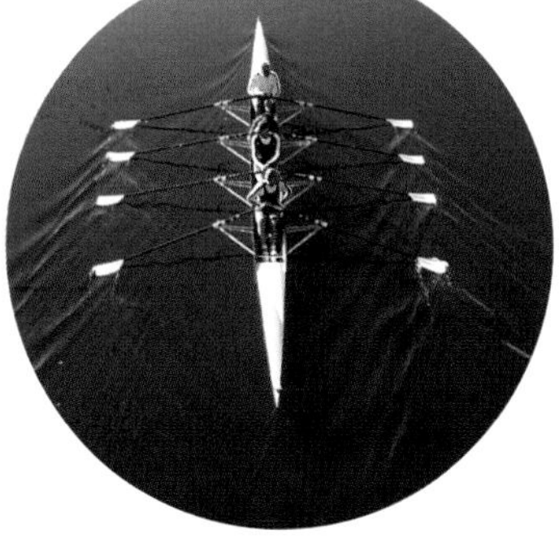

Opposite: Lendal Bridge.

INTRODUCTION

BRIDGES & TOWERS

When Skeldergate Bridge was built in 1881, the aim was to keep as much traffic as possible away from the city's narrow streets. Sailing vessels continued to load and unload their cargo at the staiths upstream and whenever a ship needed to pass, a section of the bridge was raised.

The most recent crossing to be built is the Millennium Bridge. Spanning the River Ouse between Fulford and Clementhorpe and constructed of stainless steel, this example of modern architecture stands in striking contrast to its predecessors. Far more convenient than the original rope ferry located at this point, the bridge was proposed by a group of local people keen to unite the two areas each side of the river.

Used by both pedestrians and cyclists, the opening of the bridge provided the vital link in the White Rose Cycle Route, a National Cycle Network route between Hull and Middlesbrough. This is very fitting since the revolutionary design of the bridge is said to be based on the spokes of a bicycle wheel. The Millennium Bridge is an outstanding landmark and was officially opened by Prince Andrew, the Duke of York in May 2001.

Left: Barker Tower.

Opposite: River Ouse.

Opposite bottom left & right: The Kings Arms frequently closes when the floodwater seeps over the floor of the bar. During the serious flooding of 2000, the pub got a little more than expected!

Barker tower

Situated on the south bank of the Ouse and close to Lendal Bridge is Barker Tower. A medieval watchtower, it was linked at one time with Lendal Tower on the opposite side of the river by a heavy chain. This would be raised to prevent boats from entering the city without paying a toll and also as a form of defence during times of war. Over the years, Barker Tower has had numerous uses not least, during Victorian times, as an overflow for the local mortuary.

Immediately downstream of Ouse Bridge, on opposite sides of the river, lie King's Staithe (meaning the King's landing place) and Queen's Staithe (meaning the Queen's landing place). The word 'staithe' is of Viking origin and for centuries, these quays were the bustling centre of York's trading activities. Some of the riverside warehouses of Queen's Staithe still stand, while King's Staithe has been transformed into a delightful promenade around the picturesque half-timbered pub, The King's Arms. The pub's position, just yards from the river, makes it vulnerable to periodic flooding. A yardstick mounted in the bar records the levels of some of the famous floods of the past. After heavy rain, the Ouse can rise with alarming speed and many a time, shoppers have returned to their cars parked on King's Staithe to find them awash!

RIVER OUSE, BRIDGES & TOWERS

9

WALLS & BARS

The medieval walls encircling the city provide over two miles of traffic free sightseeing. High above the thronging pavements and private gardens, a stroll on even a short section of these fortifications will provide one of the few opportunities to enjoy views of this enchanting city from a different perspective. Access is via flights of narrow steps at numerous points around the perimeter.

There is sometimes confusion over the age of the walls with many believing them to be of Roman origin. While some remains of the original Roman fortifications have survived, the bulk of what can be seen today dates from the 13th and 14th centuries.

These walls are the longest and best preserved in the country which, considering the city's turbulent history, is testament to their remarkable architecture. Built of limestone, they are set, for most of their length, on grassy embankments which in springtime are awash with daffodils.

The four main bars (or gates) of the city - Walmgate, Micklegate, Bootham and Monk Bar, are largely intact and remain potent reminders of a time when, after London, York was the most important city in the country - a time when the fear of attack was very real. There is also a fifth medieval Bar – the much smaller Fishergate Bar, and a 19th century gateway at Victoria Bar.

The gap in the wall between Red Tower and Peasholme Green denotes an area that was once so marshy that it provided an impregnable obstacle to attackers making fortification unnecessary.

The walls and bars retained a civic prominence well into the 1700s but by the 19th century whole sections of the walls had crumbled and the bars were plastered with handbills and posters. In the 1830s a section of walling at St Leonard's Place was demolished to build the Georgian Crescent. The demolition of three barbicans led to protest from the citizens of York and a plan to demolish Bootham Bar was hastily abandoned

Left: Micklegate Bar. Opposite: Bar walls in Spring.

INTRODUCTION

THE BARS

Walmgate Bar is unique in that it still retains its defensive outer gate, known as a barbican. While others have survived in medieval castles throughout the country, Walmgate Bar remains the only one of its kind within a city. This narrow extension offered an extra line of defence and any aggressors who managed to penetrate the portcullis would have been bombarded at close range from above. The stonework has been heavily rebuilt after damage by cannon fire in 1644 during the Civil War siege. Although some 12th century stonework remains, most of the bar was built during the 14th century, with the barbican being a later addition. The two storey wood and plaster building tacked incongruously to the inside of the bar dates from Elizabethan times and once housed a gate-keeper.

Bootham Bar is York's oldest, with parts dating from the 11th century and stands on the site of a Roman road that once entered the city from the north-west. The bar had to be repaired following damage sustained during the Siege of York in 1644.

The city's most important bar, guarding the main road from London, was Micklegate Bar. Many kings and nobles have entered the city through its imposing archway and its Norman construction predates that of the city walls. Its upper floors were used as a prison and up until 1754, some unfortunates ended their days by being decapitated and having their heads displayed on spikes on top of the battlements. Today, Micklegate Bar houses a fascinating little museum, devoted to the city's rich history and is accessed from the city walls.

The imposing Monk Bar heralds the gateway to Goodramgate and at one time, guarded the main north-eastern road into the city. Built in the 14th century, an extra storey was added later making it, at more than 20 metres, the tallest of the city's defences. It was also the most impregnable, with a heavy wooden portcullis that could be lowered at a moment's notice. The portcullis still remains in working order and the bar is now home to the Richard III Museum, where visitors can make up their own minds about this much-maligned monarch.

Above & opposite: Monk Bar.

WALLS & BARS

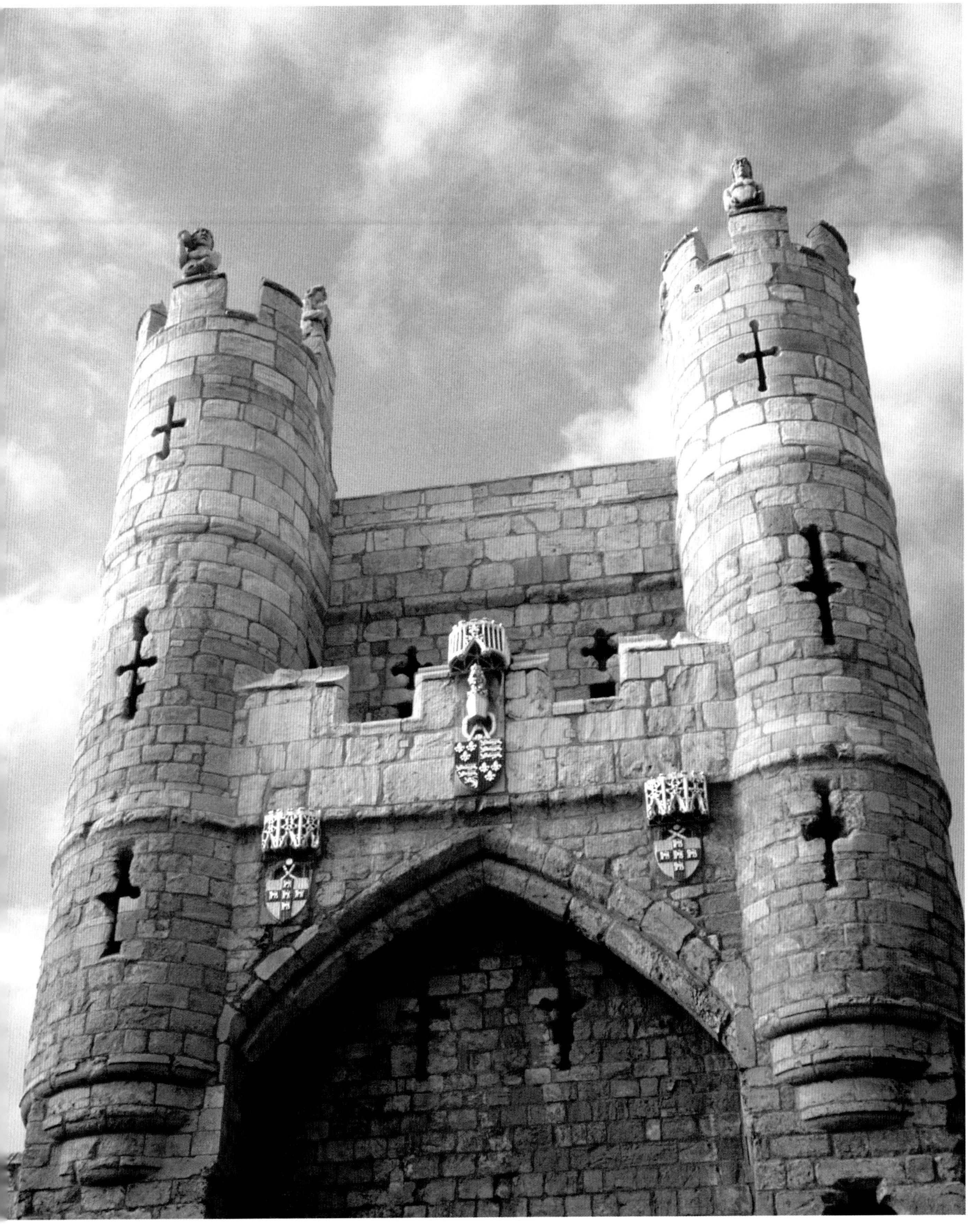

10

MEDIEVAL CHURCHES

York has a legacy of fine medieval churches. Sadly they fall within the shadow of the city's famous cathedral, often going unnoticed and overlooked by the thousands of visitors who head daily through the doors of the great Minster.

In the 1400s, York had the second largest population in the country. As attendance at church services was compulsory, it is easily understood why the city needed nearly 50 places of worship. Today, less than half of this number remain and of these, half again are redundant and used for different purposes.

For those who love quiet places, there is a handful of lovely churches that, although cannot compete with the architectural splendour of the Minster, are particularly worth exploring. Regular services are held in each except Holy Trinity.

St Denys – *Walmgate*

Off the main tourism trail, but nevertheless well worth visiting, this church has the oldest glass in York which dates back to the early 13th century. The building has had a chequered history, being damaged first during the siege of York in 1644, then by a bolt of lightning and finally by having its nave and spire demolished. Beneath the church is a medieval burial vault where members of the powerful Percy family were interred.

St Olave – *Marygate*

Occupying a delightful position near the Marygate entrance to Museum Gardens, the church of St Olave was founded in 1055 by the Scandinavian Earl Siward – hence the dedication to the patron saint of Norway. This is another church to suffer damage during the Civil War when Royalist soldiers occupied the tower and used it as a gun platform. Three hundred years ago it was virtually rebuilt with stone from neighbouring St Mary's Abbey.

INTRODUCTION, ST DENYS & ST OLAVE

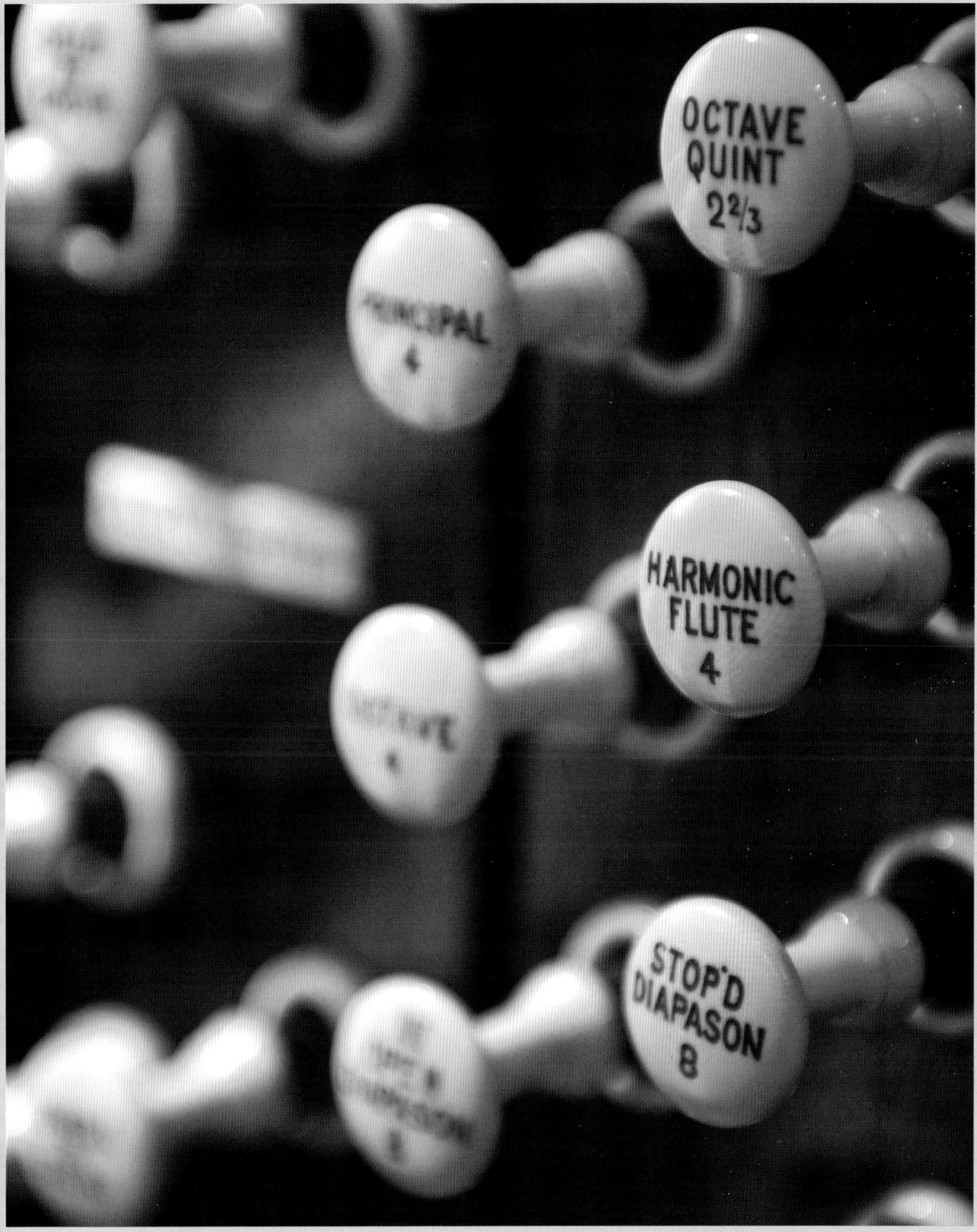

HOLY TRINITY CHURCH

Holy Trinity – *Goodramgate*

A haven of peace nestling behind busy streets, Holy Trinity is a little gem reached through a gate next to the row of medieval dwellings known as Lady Row. Dating largely from the 15th century, the church boasts a tower with a rare saddleback pitched roof, some fine stained glass in the east window and a full complement of Georgian boxed pews. This is one church that the Victorians fortunately left untouched!

The Ghost of Thomas Percy, Earl of Northumberland, is said to roam the churchyard looking for the head he lost to the executioner's axe when convicted of high treason in 1572.

Holy Trinity is one of 300 redundant churches now cared for by the Churches Conservation Trust.

MEDIEVAL CHURCHES

ALL SAINTS

All Saints – *North Street*

Of all the city's parish churches, All Saints probably retains the finest 15th century glass. Most memorable is the aisle window portraying the Six Corporal Acts of Mercy. Try to spot a figure in the Nine Orders of Angels window, wearing spectacles: an early and unusual depiction in stained glass. With a history stretching back to the 12th century, its other attractions include a slender 120-foot spire and 15th century hammer-beam roof adorned with colourful angels.

All Saints – *Pavement*

Though dating from the 14th and 15th centuries, All Saints was a site of worship from a much earlier century. It is well known as 'The Guild Church of York' because of its long association with the city's craft guilds; their shields being displayed on the south wall. A total of 39 Lord Mayors are also thought to be buried here.

The impressive lantern tower was used to provide a light to guide travellers through the Forest of Galtres which surrounded the medieval city. These days the church serves as a memorial to those who lost their lives serving their country in two world wars. Inside is a superb pulpit, medieval stained glass, an ancient lectern and a 12th century door-knocker representing the mouth of hell.

Above: A figure wearing spectacles is depicted in the stained glass of All Saints Church, North Street.

Opposite: All Saints, North Street.

MEDIEVAL CHURCHES

ST MICHAEL–LE–BELFRY

St Michael-le-Belfry – *Petergate*

St Michael-le-Belfry was named after the bell tower (belfry) of the Minster in whose imposing shadow it stands. It was rebuilt in its present form in 1525 -1536 and as such, became the last pre-reformation church to be constructed within the city. The spacious interior contains excellent examples of 18th century woodwork, including communion rails and benefaction boards. It is thought that Flemish craftsmen were responsible for the stunning 16th century glasswork.

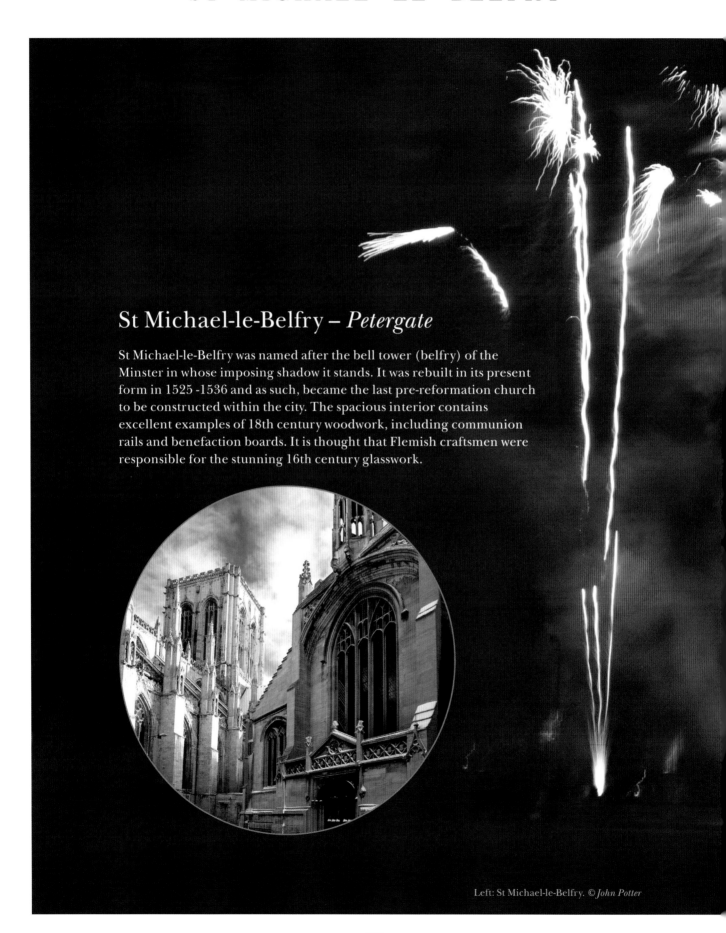

Left: St Michael-le-Belfry. ©*John Potter*

MEDIEVAL CHURCHES

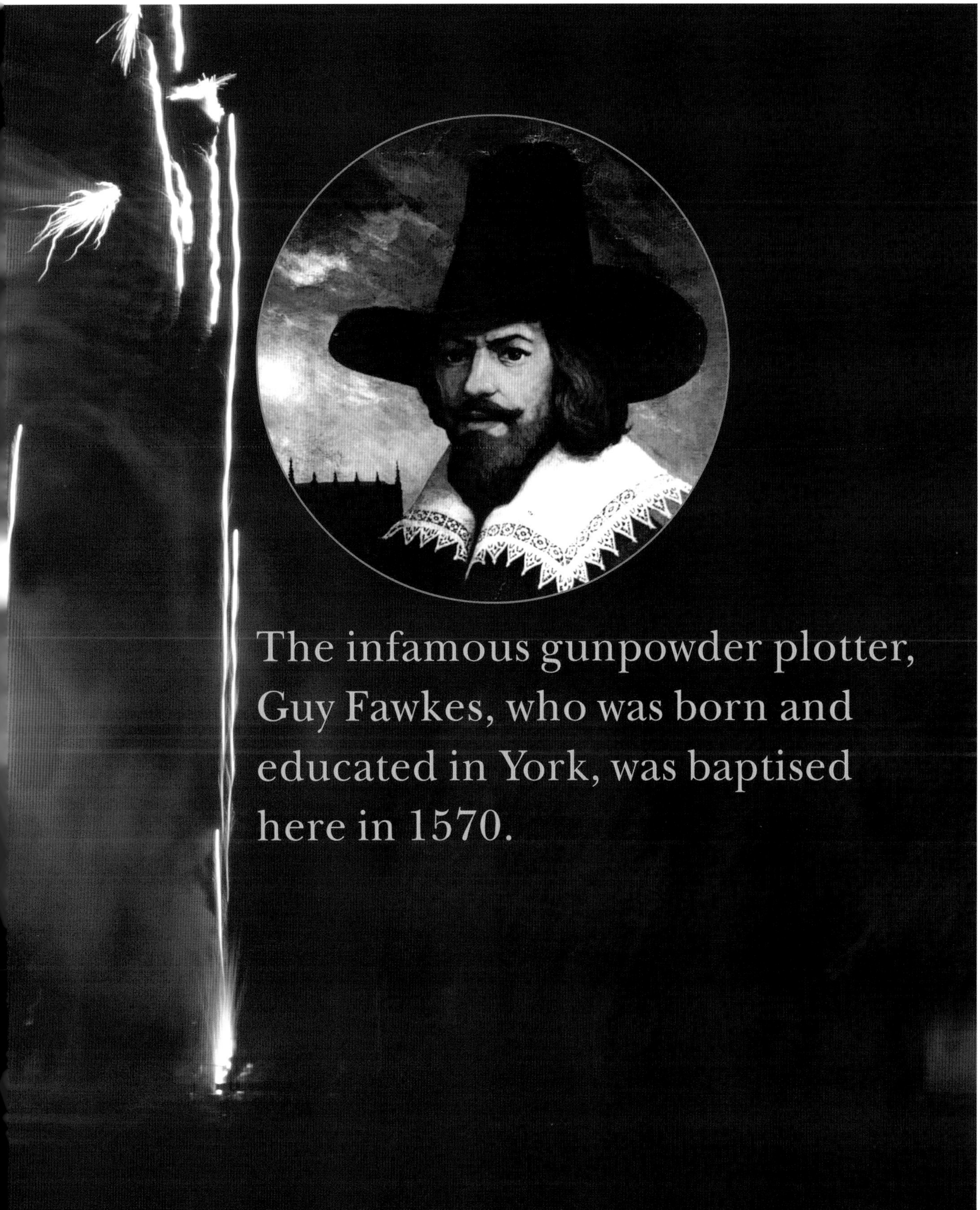

The infamous gunpowder plotter, Guy Fawkes, who was born and educated in York, was baptised here in 1570.

11

YORK MUSEUMS

INTRODUCTION

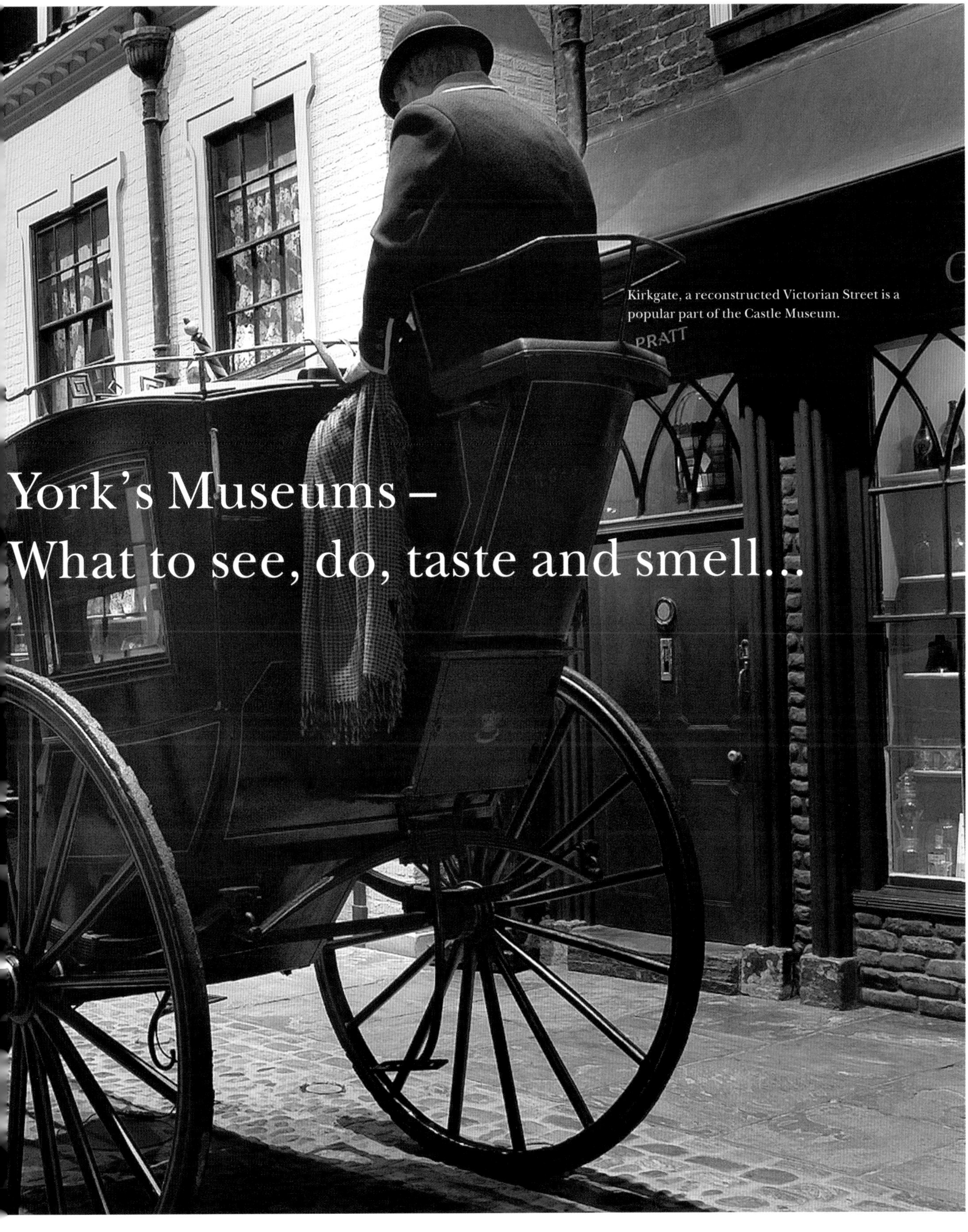

York's Museums – What to see, do, taste and smell...

Kirkgate, a reconstructed Victorian Street is a popular part of the Castle Museum.

LIVING HISTORY

The days of dull museums hoarding fusty artefacts in glass cases have, thankfully, passed. York boasts an eclectic choice of first class museums with hands-on, interactive exhibits transporting you back anything from 60 years to over 2000.

Most people know that York's **National Railway Museum** houses the finest collection of trains and loco memorabilia in the world. But how many know about the enchanting little museum at the railway station that is a mecca for railway buffs? **York's Model Railway Museum** incorporates an imaginative display of trains running along one third of a mile of OO-gauge track. Attention to detail is astonishing with over 600 model buildings, 1000 vehicles and 2,500 pocket-sized people bringing the scenery to life.

Cunningly concealed within the city's walls are two small but intriguing museums. **Micklegate Bar** and **Richard III Museum** (located in Monk Bar), depict life in medieval York. Micklegate, famous for displaying the severed heads on spikes of those unfortunate enough to be beheaded, recounts the stories of the 'heads' and who they belonged to. Richard III, at Monk Bar, as its name implies, takes visitors back to 1483 and investigates the life of the hunchback king. Was he the evil monster who murdered the little princes in the Tower of London or a courageous leader unfairly maligned by historians?

Not for the faint-hearted, the **York Dungeon** presents a somewhat scary version of historical events with all the 'horrible bits' left in. Actors, shows and special effects transport you back to some of the country's blackest and bleakest times. If, following your visit, you are in need of something to 'steady the nerves' a tour of **York Brewery** could prove to be the ideal tonic. Situated in Toft Green – just a two minute walk from Micklegate Bar, this friendly, independent brewery produces beer using traditional methods. There are frequent tours and plenty of opportunities to sample the different ales.

Situated in the shadow of Clifford's Tower, the **Military Museum** recounts the 300 year history of two famous Yorkshire regiments; The Royal Dragoon Guards and The Prince of Wales's Own Regiment of Yorkshire. Ex servicemen and women from across the world visit the museum, as is evident from the many Visitors' Books.

A few miles to the east of the city in the village of Elvington is the Yorkshire Air Museum.

A former World War II Bomber Command Station, the museum now houses over 40 aircraft – post war as well as wartime planes, and tells the story of its role in the 1939 - 45 conflict. At that time, the base was home to the only two French heavy bomber squadrons of the war and saw around 2000 French servicemen billeted in and around the city. The last German aircraft to crash on British soil was in March 1945 when a Luftwaffe fighter bomber came down in York Road.

A memorial to French airmen is situated in the village of Elvington and is a replica of the French National Air Memorial in Normandy which was erected facing towards York.

Opposite: National Railway Museum
– the largest railway museum in the world.

YORK MUSEUMS

DIGGING DOWN

....the archaeologists play their part

Over the last 30 years, digging down through layers of soil has unearthed answers to many of the city's mysteries.

And what is so exceptional about York is that there are activities where those with varying levels of interest in archaeology can get involved....

The famous interactive museum, **JORVIK Viking Centre,** was born from the astounding archaeological discovery at Coppergate in the 1970s. When developers working on a new car park and shopping precinct began to discover Viking remains, the site was handed over to York Archaeological Trust. The archaeologists couldn't believe their eyes as houses, workshops and backyards of the Viking-Age city of Jorvik were revealed. Experts excavated eight tonnes of Viking deposits and 40,000 objects preserved in the most remarkable condition. These were studied in such detail that it has enabled JORVIK to show visitors a realistic experience of Viking life.

Who knows what will be discovered at York's latest dig? The large scale, five-year excavation project at **DIG Hungate** is already uncovering fascinating finds each day and tours are available around the site.

For budding mini archaeologists, **DIG** - An Archaeological Adventure opened in 2006, invites visitors to grab a trowel and dig through the Roman, Medieval, Viking and Victorian layers to see what they can find. All the excitement without the mud - so no change of clothes necessary.

Above: DIG – An archaeological adventure.

Opposite: JORVIK Viking Centre – reconstruction of a Viking settlement.

YORK MUSEUMS

YORK'S HISTORIC SCHOOLS

Archbishop Holgate School

A former grammar school, Archbishop Holgate is a newly built school situated on Hull Road a mile from the city centre. Founded by Archbishop Holgate in 1546, the school was originally sited in Minster Close before moving to Ogleforth. In 1858 it amalgamated with the Yeoman School and was sited at Lord Mayor's Walk.

Past pupils include: Labour MP Frank Dobson.

Blue Coat School

Originally a residential school for poor boys and particularly orphans, the Blue Coat School was located at St Anthony's Hall in Peaseholme Green. It opened in 1705 along with the **Grey Coat School** for girls and was seen as the most important innovation in education in the city. The 1944 Education Act deemed that the school did not fit any of the recognised categories and was forced to close in 1947.

Bootham School

Founded in 1822 by William Simpson, the concept of a boys school had initially been the ambition of pioneering Quaker, William Tuke. Sadly, Tuke died before realising his dream but the school continued and apart from its early beginnings at the Lawrence Street home of Simpson, it has remained at its present site on Bootham since 1846. In 1899, the boys' education was interrupted when a serious fire saw them evacuated to Scarborough for three years. Today Bootham is one of the most popular co-educational independent schools in the city.

Past pupils include: Joseph Rowntree (who once lived in a house that is now part of the school), Lord Rix – actor and charity campaigner, Stuart Rose – chief executive of Marks and Spencer.

Opposite: St Peter's School.

SCHOOLS

MINSTER, MOUNT & ST PETER'S SCHOOLS

Minster School

Founded in the 7th century for the purpose of educating choristers, the school was formerly known as the Minster Song School. It went into abeyance at the Reformation and the building we see today dates only from the 1830s.

In 1987 the school became co-educational and now has 180 pupils aged from 3 – 13 and an outstanding academic as well as a musical reputation. Choristers, girls as well as boys, rehearse in the Minster each morning for one hour and then return after school to rehearse and sing evensong. They also sing on Saturdays and Sundays as well as additional religious festivals throughout the year.

St Peter's School

This independent day and boarding school claims to be the fourth oldest school in England and was originally founded with the Minster in AD627.

In 1411 it was recorded that "an occupation of the boys at St Peter's was the visiting of taverns" and, in the mid 16th century, saw one of its boys put in the stocks and beaten for playing football inside the Minster! In 1556 the School was re-founded and given a Royal Charter in new premises just off Gillygate, but these buildings were destroyed during the Siege of York and the School moved to Bedern where it stayed until circa.1730.

In 1833 it moved again into purpose-built premises (now the Minster School) before finally merging with the recently established Preparatory School on its current site in Clifton in 1844.

Former pupils include: Guy Fawkes (and four other 'Gunpowder Plotters'), cricketers Brian Sellers and Norman Yardley, television personality Harry Gration and the actor Greg Wise.

The Mount School

This independent Quaker girls' school was founded in 1785 by Esther Tuke who was headmistress until her death in 1857.Originally located in the Friend's Meeting House, it moved three times until finally, in 1857, it established itself at its present site on the Mount. The school was one of the first in York to send girls to university and remains an all girls' school for both day students and boarders.

Past pupils include: Margaret Drabble, her sister A.S. Byatt and Dame Judi Dench.

Left: The Lindley Murray Summer House in the grounds of The Mount School.

Top opposite: Choristers at The Minster School in 1989 when the road between their school and the Minster was closed to traffic. The boys no longer had to doff their caps in thanks to the motorists who stopped for them to cross.

Bottom opposite: Rowers from St Peter's on the River Ouse

YORK'S HISTORIC SCHOOLS

THE BAR CONVENT SCHOOL

For 299 years, the nuns of the Bar Convent School educated York's catholic community until the transfer of the school to the diocese in 1985.

The convent and the boarding school were founded in 1686 by Frances Bedingfield, followed by the day school in about 1696. At this time Catholic convents, Catholic education, and the celebration of Mass were still illegal, so establishing a school for Catholic girls was a dangerous venture and the early sisters risked imprisonment.

It is for this reason that when the Chapel was built in 1769, it was designed with its beautiful dome concealed beneath an ordinary slate roof. A priest's hole and ten doors were also incorporated to enable a swift exit.

In 1844 the day school was rebuilt and the central courtyard covered over with a glass roof by the architect G T Andrews who also designed York's first Railway Station. During the last war, the Convent suffered a direct hit in which five of the sisters were killed and you can still see the difference in the brickwork on Nunnery Lane where the house was rebuilt.

Today the school forms part of All Saints School but much of the Bar Convent itself remains open to the public in a different guise – the school rooms are now part of the museum and conference facilities, the sisters' rooms and school dormitories have been made into guest house rooms and the headmistress' office is now the café.

Educating York's catholic community...

Left: Ornately tiled floor at the Bar Convent.

Opposite: The Bar Convent is the oldest living convent in England.

YORK'S HISTORIC SCHOOLS

RAILWAY HERITAGE

During the Georgian era, York was a fashionable retreat for wealthy famili and because it had none of the coal deposits found elsewhere in Yorkshire the Industrial Revolution passed it by. It was only the arrival of the railway that began to transform it from a small market town into the thriving, innovative city we see today.

Much of the success of the city's fortunes can be attributed to the foresight and skulduggery of one man, an ambitious bu bullying politician George Hudson. Known as the 'Railway King', he recognised that the York of the 1820's wa in economic decline and vowed to chang its fortunes saying "I'll make all the railways come to York."

Hudson sunk a £30,000 inheritance into his railway - The York and North Midland Railway Company and by 1839, during his first tenure as Lord Mayor, the first railway line was laid – albeit only fifteen miles long. The maiden journey was accompanied by much pomp and ceremony and to ensure a good crowd, the day was made a public holiday. By the following year, a direct rail link to London was opened which meant travellers coul bid farewell to tedious and uncomfortable journeys by stage coach.

The original railway station was sited in Tanner Row and although only a terminus, required a large archway to be cut through the city wall.

Hudson's business empire expanded during the 1840's, with lines extend out from York like the spokes on a wheel. He seemed to have the Midas touch but his ruthlessness and dubious financial dealings proved to be hi downfall. By the end of that decade his corrupt business ethics had been exposed and he was forced to resign from public office and relinquish his business interests in the railway network. To compound the shame, Hudson's portrait was removed from the Mansion House and the street, once named after him, was renamed Railway Street.

Hudson died in 1871, in poverty, a forgotten man.

It took 100 years before people realised that his shortcomings were well outweighed by his huge contribution to York's prosperity and in 1971, Railway Street became known, once again, as George Hudson Street.

Above: Painting of George Hudson – the 'Railway King.' *by Francis Grant 1847*

Opposite: Before 1860, trains terminated within the city walls.

INTRODUCTION

46

RAILWAYS

By the 1860's, with York firmly established as a halfway stop on the main London – Edinburgh line, the terminus station proved to be inadequate and its replacement, the splendid building we see today, was built to a design by Thomas Prosser. Sited just outside the city wall and with a sweeping curve to take account of the bend in the river, the station is regarded as one of the finest examples of civil engineering to be built during the Victorian era. Its platform, at 1,692ft (520 metres), was the longest in England and the dramatic and innovative design, using prefabricated sections to create the huge, three-arched roof, was unveiled in 1877.

Other examples of York's fine Victorian architecture include the splendid North Eastern Railway Company's headquarters (as the company was then styled) and the original Station Hotel which got its 'Royal tag' following visits from Queen Victoria and, much later, Edward VII. Now renamed the Royal York Hotel, its popularity as a convenient rendezvous for train travellers continues.

York's famous carriage and wagon works was established in 1839 and for nearly 150 years, remained one of the city's major employers.

National Railway Museum

The first railway museum was opened in 1927 but it was many years later, with the nationalisation of the rail network, that the idea of a national railway museum was mooted. Concerted lobbying guaranteed that the museum be located in York and didn't become merely an annexe of the Science Museum in London. Opened in a redundant locomotive shed in 1975, this splendid collection of locos, rolling stock and 'railwayana' was an immediate success, chronicling almost two centuries of transport history in a series of imaginative displays.

RAILWAY HERITAGE

14

CONFECTIONERY AND THE QUAKERS

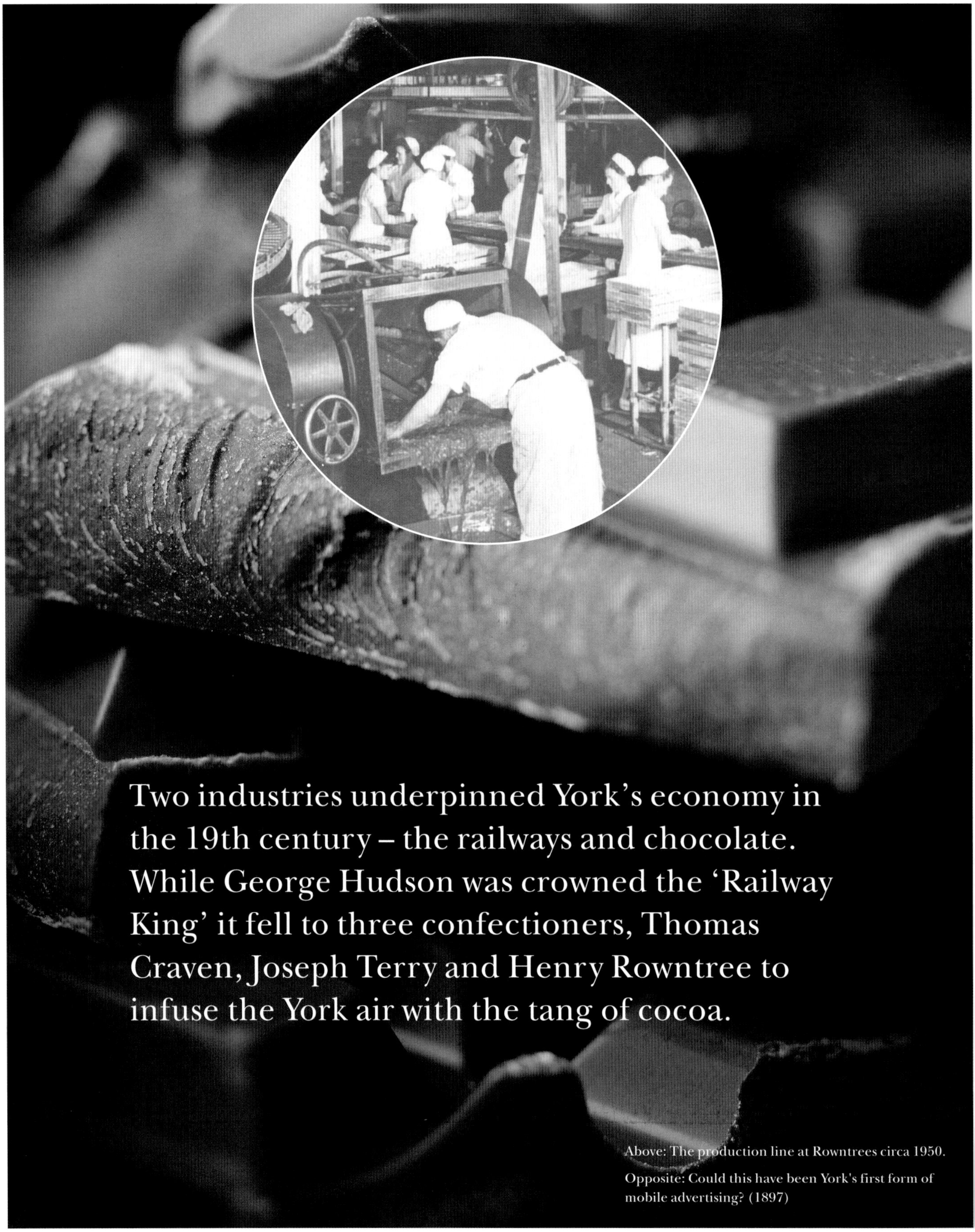

Two industries underpinned York's economy in the 19th century – the railways and chocolate. While George Hudson was crowned the 'Railway King' it fell to three confectioners, Thomas Craven, Joseph Terry and Henry Rowntree to infuse the York air with the tang of cocoa.

Above: The production line at Rowntrees circa 1950.

Opposite: Could this have been York's first form of mobile advertising? (1897)

INTRODUCTION

CONFECTIONERS

The Cravens

From as early as 1803, the Craven family were producing confectionery in York. Mary Anne Craven and her son Joseph brought international acclaim to the city when, in 1904, they bought the formula for French Sugared Almonds.The original company was sold to Bassetts in 1996.

The Terrys

A household name, synonymous with the production of Terry's Chocolate Orange, the company first began as confectioners in 1767. Originally with premises in Bootham, the firm later moved to St Helen's Square where the name can still be seen today. The mid 19th century saw Terry's supplying chocolate worldwide and by 1930 they had moved to a substantial new site on the edge of the racecourse where the clock tower became a recognised landmark. Bought by Kraft Foods in 1993, production was finally switched abroad and the York company closed down twelve years later, thereby ending nearly 200 years of chocolate-making history.

The Rowntrees

Probably one of York's most influential families with much of their legacy remaining today. As Quakers, the Rowntrees' philosophy was to care for their employees and provide a template for a lifestyle and not just employment. The company grew from simple beginnings in a small grocery shop run by Joseph Rowntree senior. In 1862 his son Henry Isaac purchased a long established confectionery business from a fellow Quaker family, the Tukes and seven years later was joined by brother Joseph. When Henry died, Joseph was left to run the factory and in 1890 his foresight led him to purchase 29 acres of land on Haxby Road. This is where he built his new factory and before long was employing 4,000 people, putting it within the top 80 manufacturing companies in the country. Employees found themselves enjoying their own sports and social clubs as well as a library, welfare officer and pension scheme – something rarely heard of in those days.

Rowntree & Co Ltd. was a household name for over one hundred years until it was purchased by the Swiss company Nestle in 1988.

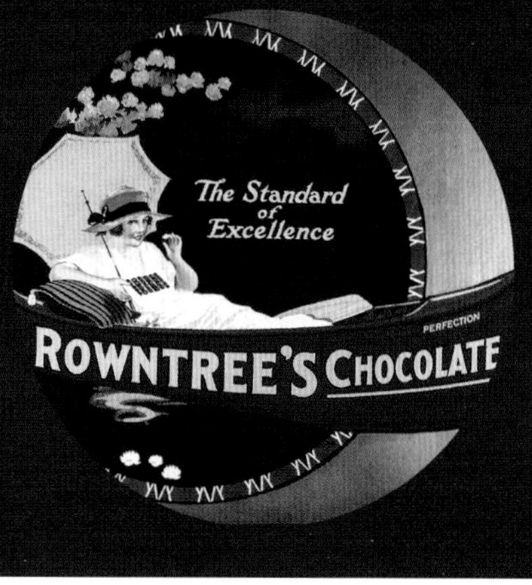

CONFECTIONERY AND THE QUAKERS

THE QUAKERS

Rowntree's Quaker beliefs

Joseph Rowntree's aim was to improve the living conditions of the whole city. He was responsible for the development of the village of New Earswick on the outskirts of York and received the Freedom of the City in 1911. When he died in 1925, he left enviable reminders of his life's work which included the founding of a school, a park and three trusts still in existence today: the Joseph Rowntree Foundation, the Joseph Rowntree Charitable Trust and the Joseph Rowntree Reform Trust.

The Quaker Influence on York

Quakers are nonconformist Christians whose regard for silent contemplation is an essential part of their worship. Officially called the Society of Friends, their unconventional spiritual trembling behaviour during meetings gave them the name 'Quakers'. Until the Act of Toleration was introduced in the late 17th century, the Quakers were persecuted because they would not attend Church of England services. On one occasion their founder, George Fox, began preaching in York Minster but was hastily evicted.

The Quakers founded a number of schools including Bootham Boys School and The Mount School for Girls. In 1796 William Tuke, a leading Quaker philanthropist started the Retreat, a hospital which remains today and was the first of its kind in the world to show compassion and care for the mentally ill.

Above: Joseph Rowntree (1836 – 1925)

Opposite top: The first Rowntree factory in Tanners Moat (1904)

Opposite bottom: Workers heading home from the new Haxby Road factory c.1953

CONFECTIONERY AND THE QUAKERS

YORK AT WAR

Throughout history, Yorkshire has been no stranger to war. When the Romans invaded in 43AD they set the scene for Britain to become one of their far flung conquests and for York, or Eboracum as it was known, to become the most northern outpost of the Roman Empire.

The later Viking invasion and capture of York in 867 resulted in Inter-marriage and conversion to Christianity, making it difficult to identify Viking from Anglo-Saxon.

The Norman invasion of 1066 completely transformed the future development of the country. The Normans defeated Harold at Hastings before conquering the rest of England. The people of York resisted fiercely and a great rebellion of 1069 resulted in the burning of the city and almost all the villages in the north. This period was known as 'the Harrying of the North'.

During the 1600s, the Civil War also took its toll on the city. Despite the powerful defences built by William the Conqueror, York fell to Cromwell's Parliamentarians, forcing the city into a negotiated but honourable surrender. This led to the end of the War and the eventual execution of Charles 1. He had made York his northern headquarters and established his printing press in St William's College.

Above: Oliver Cromwell 1599 – 1658.

Opposite: One of the city's more recent war memorials on Station Rise honours those killed in the Second World War 1939 – 1945.

INTRODUCTION

19TH AND 20TH CENTURY CONFLICTS

Until the beginning of the last century, wars and battles had been fought on terra firma (ground level). From a defence point of view, Britain's island status had protected her well.

However, the invention of the aeroplane changed all. Conflict took an unpleasant turn, bringing unexpected death and destruction to the ordinary citizen who had never signed up and who believed that the horrors of war would be somewhere else and far away.

The First World War slowly and tortuously embraced everyone. Whereas many thousands died on the battlefields of France, a new danger in the form of the Zeppelin appeared over the city's skies.

The German bombardment of York during World War I was by airships invented by Count Zeppelin in 1900. The first and most serious raid took place in May 1916 on a city unprepared and unprotected.

By the time of the second raid, York had a powerful searchlight and anti- aircraft gun in place and when the Zeppelin approached, it was chased off by anti-aircraft fire. The last raid took place in November 1916, claiming no lives and doing little damage.

Although the Great War of 1914 -18 became known as the war to end all wars, this was not to be the case and 20 years later, Britain found herself once again facing a conflict that would last six years.

The Second World War wreaked serious damage on York. The city was bombed eleven times by German planes, the most notable of these known as the Baedeker Blitz of 1942. The name 'Baedeker' comes from the guidebook which gave the cities to which it referred a star rating according to their importance. During a radio broadcast Hitler had announced his intention to bomb "certain cities in England" continuing "We shall go all out to bomb every building in Britain marked with three stars in the Baedeker Guide."

Opposite (top): World War I Zeppelin c1916.

Opposite (bottom):York railway station after the bombing in 1942. *Courtesy National Railway Museum.*

YORK AT WAR

19TH AND 20TH CENTURY CONFLICTS

During the night of April 29th 1942, the city suffered a punishing air raid. The official report states "The sirens sounded at 2.42am almost simultaneously with the dropping of the first bombs. The attack was concentrated and lasted about an hour."

Over seventy high explosive bombs and large numbers of incendiaries and magnesium flares were dropped which, with the moonlight, "Illuminated the city very effectively". There was no warning.

The German bombers – Junkers and Heinkels - flew over the North Sea to Hull and then followed the River Ouse until they reached York. Their primary target was the railway station, the carriage works, and the main lines that were vital to the movement of troops and goods. Their secondary target was Clifton Aerodrome.

When the raid started, the King's Cross to Edinburgh express was waiting in the station with civilians and soldiers sitting on board. They all found cover before a bomb hit the platform and destroyed six coaches of the train along with 20 locomotives.

Most of the east side of the city escaped damage, as did the Minster, but the church of St Martin-le-Grand in Coney Street was wrecked. The newspaper premises next door were badly hit and there were fires in New Street, Davygate, and sadly, the Guildhall was completely burnt out.

Within the city boundary, 79 people lost their lives and 238 were injured.
Over two thousand were made homeless and 9500 houses were destroyed or damaged from a total of 28,000 – one third of the city's homes.

Opposite: In 1942 German bombers struck the city and the oldest Guild Hall in the country was destroyed by fire. Someone was heard to say "Bombs had succeeded where centuries of Death Watch beetles had failed."

YORK AT WAR

NEW THREAT FOR A NEW AGE

Having withstood bows and arrows, swords and cannon fire, Zeppelins and Junkers, York was to face a further menace, but this time one that would threaten cities and nations across the world.

The Cuban Missile crisis accelerated the view that Armageddon might not be far in the future. In response to the threat of nuclear attack, a top secret Cold War Bunker was constructed in 1961. This semi-sunken bunker was sited in Acomb, one of York's suburbs, and staffed by the Royal Observer Corps. 120 volunteers trained weekly to provide vital nuclear information and fall out patterns should Britain have been targeted in the battle of the super powers.

Since being decommissioned in 1991, following the signing of a treaty between NATO and the Warsaw Pact countries, the bunker has been restored and is now managed by English Heritage. Thousands of visitors have ventured into the building's depths to gain an insight into Britain's response to rising post war tensions with the Eastern Bloc.

The threat of nuclear war prompted the launch of CND – the Campaign for Nuclear Disarmament in 1958.

Opposite: York's Cold War Bunker at Acomb.

YORK AT WAR

HERITAGE TAVERNS

...hand pulled ales and spirits!

With over 360 inns and public houses in York, it is often said that there is one for every day of the year! Whatever the reckoning, there are certainly too many to mention but too many to ignore. The only way to gain a taste of the city's hostelries is to sample just one or two....or three, or more!

A visit to the Black Swan in Peasholme Green demonstrates the meaning of 'authenticity'. It feels as if history has placed a preservation order on its medieval beams, snugs and passageways. Like all good York hostelries, this one time 16th century family residence boasts two important ingredients – good beer and ghosts.

At the opposite end of the size spectrum is a pub in Fossgate that comprises just two rooms and a drinking corridor with a folding seat. The Blue Bell has a charm of its own and is surely one of the most compact 'watering holes' in the country! However, it's the perfectly preserved Edwardian interior that makes this little pub a genuine heritage tavern, appealing not just to historians but to beer lovers who will relish the hand pulled ales.

A huge golden slipper hanging above the door advertises the name of this long frequented tavern of entertainment. Situated in Goodramgate, near to Monk Bar, the Golden Slipper has been known simply as 'the Slipper' as far back as 1818. Dating from the 15th century with a cellar that is older still, this tavern has a chequered history to match. A medieval slipper that would have been hidden in brickwork to ward off evil spirits was discovered by workmen in 1983. Like many York hostelries, this too has its own ghost and 'George', as he is known, has often made his presence felt when any changes have been made to the interior.

Walk along Stonegate, probably the loveliest street in the city and you will find the Punch Bowl. It was during the late 1600s that 'Punch Bowl' signs became politically associated with the reforming Whig party and would attract customers of the same political persuasion. Punch was the preferred drink of the Whigs whilst the Tories preferred claret. The inn has survived two fires, one of which claimed the life of its elderly landlord although his ghost is often seen descending the cellar steps.

INNS & PUBLIC HOUSES IN YORK

Inside the Blue Bell Public House – one of the most compact 'watering holes' in the country.

HISTORIC INNS OF YORK

Also in Stonegate, Ye Olde Starre Inne is probably one of the city's oldest surviving taverns. It was to here in 1644 that soldiers wounded at the battle of Marston Moor were brought for medical help. Its splendid wood panelling, open fireplaces and decorative glasswork have no doubt been witness to much of York's history.

A tavern which is deceptively large and comprises an assortment of medieval and Georgian architecture is the Old White Swan in Goodramgate. In the courtyard can still be seen the four 'mounting' steps used to mount horses. The inn has had a variety of different uses over the centuries including that of a pigsty, barber's shop, coaching house and poultry market. Records show that in 1712 it was owned by the church and paid an annual rental of just £12.

Another hostelry worth exploring in Goodramgate is the Snickleway Inn. Dating from the 15th century, its medieval timbers, cosy rooms and roaring fires make this a welcome sanctuary on a chilly day. A ten minute walk away, the imposing Red Lion on Merchantgate is a magnificently preserved timber frame building dating from the 15th century; although a fireplace and bread oven, believed to be much older, have recently been discovered. This tavern would have been conveniently situated for the medieval merchants and those trading at the nearby pig market. Legend has it that the notorious highwayman, Dick Turpin, who was hanged in York in 1739, made one of his escapes from an upper floor window.

A lovely colonnaded doorway marks the entrance to Thomas's on Museum Street. Formerly known as Etridge's Royal Hotel, it had, in the past, been a more substantial building and a popular choice of hostelry with the racing fraternity who stabled their horses at the rear.

Archives show that the Golden Fleece on Pavement was an inn as far back as 1667 and as such, remains one of the oldest taverns in the city. Once owned by the merchant adventurers who were responsible for the woollen trade, its name signifies the importance of the industry. The timber frame construction and lack of foundations cause the unevenness of its floors and where the beer garden now stands, horses were once stabled. The yard at the rear is named after Lady Alice Peckett whose husband John was Lord Mayor of York and also owner of the inn at the beginning of the 18th century. According to many resident guests, Alice Peckett is one of five 'people' to still wander the endless corridors and staircases.

Above: A huge golden slipper hangs above the door of the pub by the same name on Goodramgate.

Opposite: The Golden Fleece on Pavement.

The Punch Bowl on Stonegate.

HERITAGE TAVERNS

HISTORIC INNS OF YORK

Lendal Cellars stands on the site of an Augustine Friary that was founded in 1272 but fell victim to the Dissolution of the Monasteries. During the early 1700s, most of the area was owned by the Oldfield Family who developed a flourishing wines and spirits business. Today, the Cellars still bear ample evidence of many wine bins for the storage of bottles and also thralls, upon which stood casks of wine which were allowed to mature prior to bottling. In the corner of the cellars there remains a bricked up chimney which provided ventilation for a sub cellar below. There is an unconfirmed belief that there was originally a passage between the sub-cellar and the river for the purpose of conveying casks of wine and spirits directly from the river to the premises.

During alterations to convert the cellars into a pub, builders discovered remains of a much older construction, along with the uncovering of a human adult skeleton, perhaps further evidence of a friary.

The 300 year old Three Tuns in Coppergate is yet another timber framed hostelry with quaint nooks and crannies. Its name derives from the old coat of arms of the Vintners or wine makers with a 'tun' being the largest component.

Just how big is a tun?

Firkin 9 gallons

Keldekin 18 gallons

Barrel 30 gallons

Househead 54 gallons

Tun 216 gallons or

1728 pints!

Opposite page: Lendal Cellars.

HERITAGE TAVERNS

HAUNTED YORK

Nowhere in Britain is the visitor's appetite for ghost stories better satisfied than here in York.

Heralded as being the most haunted city in Europe, guided ghost walks set off each evening around the narrow streets and snickelways in search of the supernatural, hearing tales of the city's gruesome past and unexplained sightings.

One of the most famous stories centres on an apprentice heating engineer, Harry Martindale who, in 1953 was working in the cellar of Treasurer's House when he heard the sound of a horn. Through the wall emerged a ragged legion of Roman soldiers, led by a centurion on horseback. They crossed the floor and disappeared through the far wall, appearing to have no feet and their legs cut off at the knees. Martindale was so terrified that it was many years before he mentioned the sighting. The description of the soldiers' uniform was of a style unknown to historians, but after considerable research it was discovered that their description matched that of 4th century Roman legionaries. They would have been following a Roman road that at one time ran under the house some 18 inches lower than the cellar floor.

The title for the most haunted building in York might well go to King's Manor. Built 750 years ago as part of nearby St Mary's Abbey, there have been reports of eerie cries and sightings including the vision of a monk and a woman dressed in a green, Tudor style dress clutching a spray of roses.

The battle of Marston Moor in 1644 was fought between Oliver Cromwell's Roundheads and an army of Cavaliers led by Prince Rupert. About 6,000 men perished on that fateful day as Cromwell's forces routed the Cavaliers. Many of the wounded were brought to King's Manor to have their wounds dressed. Their groans of pain have been heard in the main courtyard and also in the cellar of Ye Olde Starre Inne, which became a makeshift operating theatre after the battle.

Above: King's Manor – renowned for its Tudor ghosts!

INTRODUCTION

Shambles. Each evening ghost walks set out across the city regaling stories of unexplained sightings.

GHOSTS OF YORK

The now-redundant Church of the Holy Trinity in Goodramgate is supposed to be haunted by the headless ghost of Thomas Percy, 7th Earl of Northumberland. He was executed for treason in 1572, having rebelled against Elizabeth I. His head was displayed on a pole on top of Micklegate Bar to discourage other dissidents but his body was buried in the churchyard. His ghost is said to wander between the gravestones, as though searching for his missing head.

A sad medieval tale is attached to Holy Trinity Church in Micklegate concerning a couple living nearby. The husband died in an accident and was buried in the churchyard, leaving his wife with their only child. To compound the woman's grief, her child succumbed to an outbreak of the plague and, to prevent the spread of the disease, was buried in unsanctified ground outside the city walls. Twice bereaved, the woman herself soon died and was buried next to her husband leaving her troubled spirit to wander the area, searching for the child she lost.

Public Houses *with spirit*

One of the many pubs said to be haunted – and certainly one of the oldest in the city, is the **Black Swan** in Peasholme Green. A regular visitation is by a beautiful young woman in a long white dress who is seen staring distractedly into the fireplace. There is also a man who, by the cut of his clothes and his bowler hat, belongs to Victorian times. He appears to be waiting impatiently for someone but gradually his apparition fades away.

In Stonegate, **Ye Olde Starre Inne** has also had its fair share of sightings. In addition to the piteous cries of wounded soldiers, two black cats have been seen on numerous occasions as has the ghost of an old lady making her way slowly up the stairs, though this apparition is only ever seen by young children.

The Cock and Bottle in Skeldergate has a ghost identified as George Villiers, the 2nd Duke of Buckingham, who lived during the reign of Charles II and has shown himself on many occasions. He led a rakish life marked by a number of affairs that scandalised the King's court and was the original Georgie Porgie of the children's rhyme who..... 'kissed the girls and made them cry'. His ghost still haunts the pub, but appears only to women – sometimes even fondling them!

The Snickleway Inn on Goodramgate has a history of hauntings. On the top floor is an evasive ghost whose presence is marked only fleetingly by the scent of lavender. The friendly ghost of a Victorian child has been seen sitting on the stairs, but more mischievous is a spirit that has been known to turn off the beer taps in the cellar.

A phantom figure has made a number of appearances at the **York Arms,** opposite the Minster, though accounts of the sightings have varied from that of a child to an elderly woman. Objects have been known to move and doors open and close as if by some unseen hand.

The cells to a Victorian police station on Parliament Street were witness to an unpleasant incident in 1865. The building above is said to be haunted by Benjamin Wallis who, following arrest on trumped-up charges, was suffocated in one of the police cells.

HAUNTED YORK

Black Swan, Peasholme Green.

ORPHANS, THE GREY LADY & THE CAVALIER

In the mid 19th century, Bedern, just off Goodramgate, became the site of a workhouse for orphans known as the York Industrial Ragged School. The master was paid to take in local orphans and street children, giving them work in exchange for food and clothing. Unfortunately he was a cruel, heartless man who kept their earnings for himself and watched them slowly die of cold and starvation. Too lazy to dispose of the bodies, he would lock the corpses in a cupboard until the stench of rotting flesh forced him to bury them. During the harsh winters the frozen ground made this impossible and as the months passed, the master became convinced that he could hear screams emanating from the padlocked cupboard. They played on his guilty conscience so much that he was driven mad and taking a huge knife, he charged through the school massacring the remaining children. He was found the next morning, weeping over the bloody bodies of the children and sent off to the local asylum where he lived out the rest of his days.

The spirits of the dead children are sometimes heard in this area playing and laughing. However, if you listen for long enough, the playful laughter changes into screams of terror.

The Grey Lady
takes her curtain call

A room behind the dress circle of the Theatre Royal is said to be haunted by the Grey Lady, a medieval nun who was punished for falling in love with a young nobleman. The room was part of St Leonard's, a hospital run by a strict order of monks and nuns, and when the affair was discovered, she was thrown into a windowless room which was bricked up, effectively burying her alive.

To this day, the room retains a cold and eerie atmosphere and the appearance of this peaceful woman, dressed in her faded grey habit, is said to be a good omen for the theatre's current production.

And finally....
does your hair stand on end?

Staff and clients of a hairdressing salon in High Petergate say that unexplained occurrences are often happening. Magazines are thrown on the floor, the kettle is switched off and cupboards left open. Staff admit to seeing a shadow on the stairs. Further research has revealed that a firm of surveyors who occupied the building in the 1980s employed a cleaner who was heard to exclaim that while she was happy in her work, she "didn't care much for the man with the feather in his hat who kept watching her!" More recent occupants of the building recalled seeing, on numerous occasions, a Cavalier standing on the stairs. Perhaps he waits, hoping to have his hair cut!

HAUNTED YORK

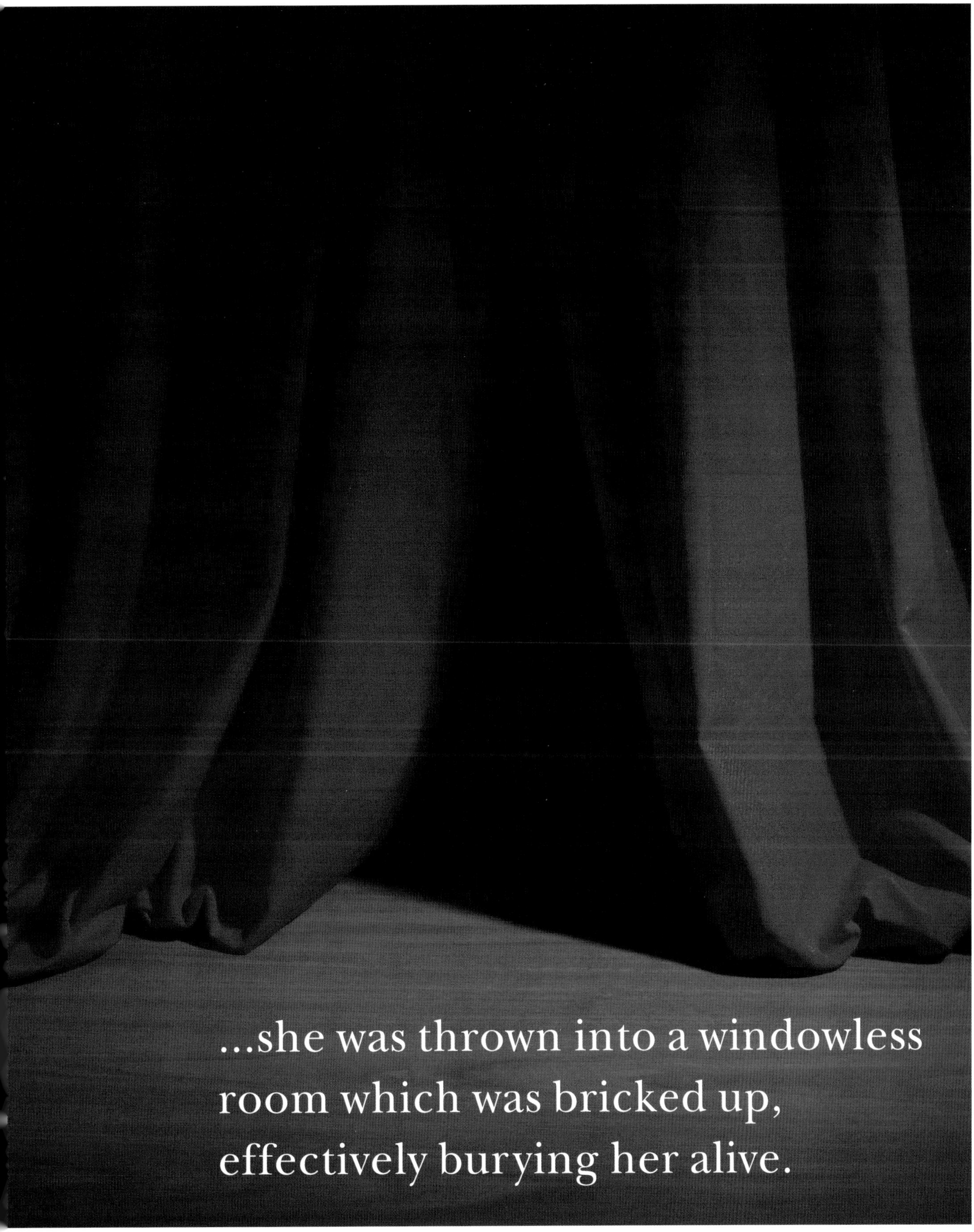

...she was thrown into a windowless
room which was bricked up,
effectively burying her alive.

ACKNOWLEDGMENTS & IMAGES

Pages 4&5. The City Walls. *Courtesy Yorkshire Tourist Board.*

Page 6. Actress Dame Judi Dench who received an Oscar for her role in the film 'Shakespeare in Love'. ©*York and County Press.*

Page 7. The Minster in Autumn. © *Paul Crossman.*

Pages 10 & 11. Painting by Henry Cave of the original Ouse Bridge as it would have looked in 1809. *Courtesy City of York Council.*

Page 16. Head of Constantine. *Courtesy York Museums Trust.*

Page 18. 8th Century Copper Helmet. *Courtesy York Archaeological Trust.*

Page 19. Virgin and Child. *Courtesy Dean and Chapter of York and Jarrold Publishing.*

Page 20. Viking coins. *Courtesy York Archaeological Trust.*

Page 21. Celebrating the Viking Festival. © *Ken Shelton.*

Pages 22 & 23. Unusual perspectives of Clifford's Tower taken from a micro air balloon by remote controlled camera. ©*John Jones, Skycell.*

Page 28. Close helmet. *Courtesy York Museums Trust.*

Page 29. The Surrender of York to the Roundheads by Ernest Crofts. *Courtesy Sotherby's Picture Library.*

Page 50. Line drawing taken from the book A Walk Around the Snickelways. *Courtesy Mark Jones.*

Page 65. Anglo Saxon gravestone. © *Dean and Chapter of York Minster.*

Pages 66 and 67. The York Minster Fire. © *York and County Press.*

Pages 68 & 69. *Courtesy Cityscape Maps Ltd.*

Page 80. Dr John Sentamu. *Courtesy of the Archbishop's Office.*

Pages 98 & 99. Treasurer's House. ©*NTPL/Nick Meers www.nationaltrust.org.uk*

Page 105. The Kings Arms at full flood. ©*York and County Press.*

Page 116. Cameo image showing St Michael-le-Belfry. © *and courtesy John Potter. www.jpotter-landscape-photographer.com*

Page 125. *Courtesy St Peter's School.*

Page 126. *Courtesy The Mount School.*

Page 127. Top: ©*York and County Press.* Bottom: *Courtesy St Peter's School.*

Page 131. *Courtesy Nestle Confectionery Ltd. (Rowntree).*

Page 134 & 135. *Courtesy Nestle Confectionery Ltd.*

Pages 136 & 137. *Courtesy York Museums Trust.*

Page 138. Joseph Rowntree. *Courtesy The Joseph Rowntree Foundation.*

Page 139. Top: *Courtesy Nestle Confectionery Ltd. (Rowntree)*
Bottom: *Courtesy City of York Council.*

YORK SOUVENIR GUIDE

Page 143. Top: *Courtesy Yorkshire Air Museum.*
Bottom: *Courtesy National Railway Museum Archive.*

Page 145. *Courtesy City of York Council.*

Project coordination and management: Rachel Norris & Sue Frumin at Visit York.

Our thanks to designer Justin Burns and photographer Gareth Buddo for their unstinting support, patience and good humour.

Justin Burns Design
mail@justinburnsdesign.co.uk

Furmoto Photography
www.furmoto.com

Every effort has been made to ensure that the content of this publication is accurate. To the best of our knowledge all copyright holders have been contacted. Any oversights or errors are entirely unintentional. Please notify us in writing or via email so that amendments can be made in future editions. Email: admin@visityork.org.

VisitYork

Supported by
YORKSHIRE FORWARD
The Region's
Development Agency